Contents

1 feijão . arroz . mango salsa . picante   5

2 zucchini steaks . coconut-wheat bread . passionfruit hummus . tomato salad   19

3 stirfried vegetables . coconut polenta . cabbage slaw   37

4 chana masala . chapattis . cilantro-peanut chutney . carrot salad . raitu   53

5 veggie burgers . buns . ratatouille . carrot mayonnaise . condiments   65

6 stuffed peppers . couscous . roasted tomato salsa   77

7 squash and potato empadas . pico de gallo . carrot hummus   87

8 beet soup . texas caviar   101

9 some brasilian favorites   107

1.1 red rice

according to the kama sutra, if i recall, there are sixty-four tasks or talents a courtesan must be able to perform with superior skill, and *one* of them is to prepare rice in 40 different ways. the most simple – no matter what your color or size of rice is — is boiling.

- 1 cup of rice
- 2 cups of water

the longer and browner (the more hull each grain has, the more mass, the more density) your rice, the more water you will need. really short white rounded grains (which you shouldn't really be using if you have a choice) will need less. so a really long grain brown rice could take $2\frac{1}{2}$ cups of water, and sushi rice takes just $1\frac{1}{2}$.

IT DOESN'T REALLY MATTER THOUGH because this method replaces the care of measuring with the care of attention. once you've figured it out for your particular rice you can resume the cruise control you've been c(l/r)utching this whole damn time.

if the rice looks like it might have some teeth-breaking rocks in it, like the organic red rice we bought in brasil, sift through it in a pizzapan to remove any offenders. if it looks web-y, dirt-y, or otherwise like it came directly from the earth, rinse it.

place it with the water to boil on high heat. i add a little bit of fat (oil or butter) and salt. this serves to keep the rice from sticking and to bring out a bit of flavor, but mainly it's a ritual. you can add anything you want — cloves, soy sauce, bacon bits, whatever.

when the water boils, reduce the heat to a simmer and cover. the rice will steam and absorb the water. if you have done the proportions perfectly, after a certain mystical amount of time

a) all the water will be gone
b) the rice will be perfectly cooked

most likely this will not be the case. when you check (and don't wait too long because you can't unburn it), you will compare the amount of water left with the amount the rice needs to cook. if it's basically done and there's still water swishing around, all you have to do is pour the water out of the pan and set it back to keep cooking. if the water's almost gone and the rice is still raw, all you have to do is add some water. it helps to add the water in small batches so it can be heated without lowering the temperature of the rice too much.

since you've already ruined the steampressure situation by checking the rice, take a few seconds to stir it against burning or sticking. you'll get a good sense of its moisture as you do this.

know that even after you turn the heat off the rice will continue to cook and absorb a little more water, so if you check it a little later, it's already done and there's a bunch of water, EVERYTHING WILL BE ALL RIGHT. drain the rice well (use a strainer if you have to) and then set it back in the pan with the lid on to finish. don't check it again until you eat to demonstrate your faith.

1.1.1 the *pattern* underneath arroz vermelho

- the basic outline for boiling rice is:

    1. heat an empty pan
    2. add some sort of lubricant
    3. add the rice
    4. add the liquid (usually 2:1) with salt
    5. turn down the heat when the water is boiling; cover
    6. let steam to perfection, turn off, fluff.

- in a standard boiled rice you don't necessarily have to add butter or oil (step 2) though it does help with sticking, especially for white rice (more glutinous).

- in between many of these steps you can add spices or other vegetables to cook with your rice. they should be added according to hardness — potatoes at the beginning, greens at the end. spices which require browning can be added between steps 2-3 to roast and release their flavors into the oil.

- remember that you can mix different types of rice together, or even rice with other grains (see chapter six). also, keep your mind open to the notion that liquid is not necessarily synonymous with water: you can use old soup, vegetable stock, the cooking water from beets or potatoes, some milk, coconut milk, tea, coffee etc. alcohol is also popular (like in risotto), and while i've never found much of a taste difference, it looks great on a menu (... accompanied by a georgian wild rice earnestly simmered in a white wine reduction ...)

- soaking the rice for a few hours (or overnight) will greatly reduce the cooking time, because the rice will already have absorbed a significant amount of water. it's another way that a little bit of work (perhaps 30 seconds) the night before can save you ten minutes of cooking while hungry the next day. this is a cornerstone of my argument against the supposed economy of "fast food" — the food is not actually cooked or prepared any faster; *you*, as a narrow alienated individual, have to deal with it less. to compete with that mentality (and compete we should, because who wants to wait an hour for dinner after spending all day working for the man), you must learn a handful of slight and clever tricks to save yourself that precious illusion they call time. all this and more in pamphlet "how and why to fuck the system by cooking your own food (and your neighbors' goddammit)", coming out later on in the kaliyuga.

1.1.2 variations on red rice

clove or cinnamon pulão

the first and simplest rice i learned how to make was an indian pulão, which follows the technique outlined above with these variations —

- use long grain basmati rice if you can get it
- the rice is generally soaked and rinsed ahead of time
- one uses ghee in step 2
- you throw in a few whole black peppercorns and whole cloves with the rice and water

this can also be made with brown basmati. it has the perfumed aroma of the basmati with added sweet accents of black pepper and clove.

cinnamon perfumed rice is made in a similar way, except that i'll sauté a cinnamon stick (broken into two or three removable pieces) in the butter for a few minutes before adding the rice and water. for an added kick you can add a $\frac{1}{2}$ teaspoon of ground cinnamon to the water as well.

my mom will typically stir in a little butter at the end and if you're ever trying to impress some non-vegans, you should follow her lead.

magic yellow rice

this simplest variation is merely to add $\frac{1}{2}$ teaspoon of turmeric to the water when cooking any white rice. turmeric is a powerful spice, medicine, and dye, and even a tiny amount will dye the entire pot of rice yellow, a boon for those mindful of plating aesthetics.

magic purple rice

another simple variation puts one diced beet into the water with the rice. the cooking beet will turn the entire pot of rice purplecolor!purple, which most people have never even imagined, must less witnessed, in their mortal histories. the sweet beet flavor goes well with the clove/pepper pulão variation above.

sweet potato biriyani

sweet potatoes were always in the market, though never very good. but sometimes you get tired enough to use them. this recipe works equally well with yams, and likely tastes much better.

- 1 large starchy tuber

- 1 carrot
- 2 cups of rice
- 4 cups of water
- 3 bay leaves
- 2 tablespoons of raw peanuts
- cinnamon
- clove
- black pepper
- butter or oil

prepare to boil the rice as suggested above. grind together the spices (or get them ground if you don't have the means of production to do it at home) and sauté them for a minute in the butter. add the rice and stir well with the butter and spices, allowing it to toast lightly before adding the liquid. with the liquid add the sweet potato, chopped into bite-sized chunks, as well as the bay leaves and peanuts. when the rice reaches a boil add the carrot in small diced cubes, simmer down, and cover.

fatty coconut rice

replace half of your cooking water with coconut milk, stir well in the beginning to avoid scorching, and cook normally. adding a bit of mango purée or diced mango will give added sweetness and bring further to mind the Absolute Perfection of the tropical world. a bit of toasted coconut or almond makes an excellent garnish.

for a fatty rice experience without the coconut pricetag, try using milk, half and half, evaporated milk, or condensed milk for some fraction of the cooking liquid.

spanish-style fried rice

there are two types of rice commonly called fried rice. the first one rolls the rice around, still dry, with spices and onions to the point of browning, then dramatically takes down the temperature using the cooking liquid.

- 1 diced onion
- some celery (optional)
- a mix of cayenne pepper, cumin, paprika, and oregano
- 2 cups of rice
- 4 cups of water
- salt

use something closer to a frypan than a pot for this variation. start by heating one tablespoon of oil in the pan and add the rice when hot. continue to flip and stir the rice, coating it with the oil. when it starts to look a little drier, add the spices and stir together. as the temperature will be hot, they should release their flavors and start to perfume quickly. when the rice begins to brown, add your onion and celery. this will take down the heat a little bit, buying more time for the onions to cook and the spices to develop before the rice wants to burn. when the rice starts to brown yet again, add the cooking liquid. using vegetable stock or chopped tomatoes (maybe from a can, even!) makes an appreciable difference. simmer when it boils and stir occasionally — the tomatoes and red spices should give the familiar orange color.

the cheesily minded should not pass up the opportunity to sprinkle the rice with cheese when it's almost done, and either cover or broil to melt it.

chinese-minded fried rice

this recipe follows the second type of fried rice i have encountered. it's a recycling process of yesterday's dinner into today's lunch, and the only chinese connection i can imagine is that it works best with soy sauce.

- leftover rice
- some cooking oil
- onions
- garlic
- soy sauce
- sesame seeds
- perhaps an egg

heat oil in a pan and chop your onions and garlic. fry them on medium heat until translucent. while they are frying add a little water and soy sauce to the rice container and break up the chunks with your fingers. when the onions are translucent add the rice and turn up the heat, stirring vigorously to separate the rice and mix well with your spices. if you eat eggs, break in an egg or two at the end, throw in a couple shakes of sesame seeds, and continue cooking (back to medium heat) until done.

this is an excellent rice to accept chopped greens (spinach, beet greens, chard) as well, just before you would add the egg.

fluff and garnish with finely chopped green onions before serving.

1.2   refried red beans

ajwain/ajmoda is an indian herb that i've seen explained as oregano seed, thyme seed, and celery seed. it's likely something else entirely. i have found that it goes quite well with the excruciatingly popular cooking oil of bahia, dendê. azeite-de-dendê is made from little black olive looking berries clustered around the trunk of a palm tree. it has a reputation for being fatty and unhealthy, which translates to a spicy heavy flavor, a strong aromatic presence, and a deep red color.

- some tablespoons azeite-de-dendê
- some tablespoons ajwain seeds
- one medium onion, chopped, for each cup of cooked beans
- many cups of cooked red beans (red pinto looking creatures)
- some ground cumin (optional)

pcook the red beans (see explanation below) and drain them. this would of course work with any bean but the whole red thing wouldn't fly as smoothly. heat a saucepan that can take some punishment, to the high side of the fire. when it's hot add enough dendê oil such that it lightly covers the bottom of the pan.

toss in the seeds and let them sizzle and pop. their flavor will fill your kitchen and when it does (but before they blacken) add the chopped onions. fry them vigorously and attentively on high heat until they brown. if they start to stick or otherwise don't seem right before they get to be browning, add some more dendê. when the onions are literally brown you can add the cumin. doing so will make the flavor more familiar and likable — the ajwain can be strong and foreign on its own. remember to brown the cumin, cooking it on high heat until you are shocked by the pungency of its aroma, before you add the beans.

now add even more dendê with the beans and stir everything together. reduce the heat to medium and spend the next few moments of your life BEING the mixing and crushing of those beans. no bean left intact: some a paste and most mere fractions of their harvested selves. this is the well-frying of the beans, where they come face to face with the vermilion specter of dendê, absorb the depth and pungency of the spices, and evolve into the alreadiness they have been awaiting.

salt to taste, serve.

1.2.1 the *pattern* of refrying beans

the first thing the people need to know, before they take either control, the streets, or the power, is how to cook beans. somewhere in this book there is a section on Equipment and therein lies the answer.

once you have quickly- and safely-cooked beans, and forever evicted the twin scourges of tin cans and excessive flatulence from your hallowed kitchen, you can start getting into the wonderful world of leguminous protein in all its protean variations.

the frijol refrito is probably (and justifiably) the most famous of these. a typical refried-bean pattern (USE THIS FOR ANY and EVERY DRIED BEAN) goes something like this

1. pcook your beans
2. while they are cooking
   (a) chop some sort of onion
   (b) prepare (usually roast and grind) some sort of spice
   (c) heat oil in hot pan (medium-high)
   (d) fry onions until browned
   (e) release pressure from cooker (it should be done)
   (f) fry spices until smelly
   (g) add beans, saving water off to the left
   (h) cook together with low heat and high energy, mashing until it looks like it came out of a cheap can
   (i) add last minute touches and salt.

note that:

- indians put a small amount of asafoetida (which tastes horrible) with all beans as a digestive aid.

- most beans go well with garlic, which should be added as the onions show evidence of browning.

- each bean goes well with some spices/herbs and not others. let reckless experimentation be your guiding star.

- final elements often include cilantro, lemon juice, salt, and sugar; important additions for the palate that neither want nor need to be heated.

1.2.2 variations on refried beans

refried feijão fradinho *dip*

use the pattern above.

so for the feijão fradinho that are so ubiquitous in bahia, i applied this technique to green onions (excising the root end and the sad looking sections of the top), fenugreek seeds and garlic. to be precise, i threw the garlic in between steps (d) and (f) while i performed (e) with my other hand. it's an advanced maneuver.

fenugreek is an indian plant and you'll have to BUY the hard angular seeds from an ETHNIC store. they are too hard to use raw and turn soft and pleasant (and bitterly toned) when dry roasted, allowing easy grinding. if the last sentence really turned you off, you can use cumin but cumin is such a staple spice with this sort of dish so please for the love oflove!for the love of martha try something else. i imagine dill- and pumpkin-seed would both give interesting flavor experiences.

for the final touches, chopped cilantro and lime juice are essential as few other things in this world.

a note on nomenclature: this is a dip, not a plate of beans. why? essentially it comes down to the power structure appropriating language to manipulate those among us who recognize it only on the level of a communication tool and neglect to notice the deep mindwarp-level where it really simmers.

specifically, you've mashed the beans enough to kill any agency or identity in- and for-themselves, so they just default to a mashy hive-mind we call 'dip'. the consistency is thick and starchy enough to balance heftily on a bread or chip, and the spicing a bit too prominent to be a main dish anywhere outside of the indian hypercontinent.

standard and delicious black beans

use plenty of garlic when the onions are browning and add the following spices when the garlic browns:

- lots of ground cumin
- oregano
- chopped rosemary (optional)

brown well until mighty and fragrant. when you add the beans use some of the reserve liquid (and perhaps a chopped tomato) as well to provide a lounge for a couple of bay leaves. simmer down the water for ten minutes, allow the bay leaves to express themselves before removal and mashing begins in earnest.

these are excellent with finely chopped onions and cilantro mixed in at the end, perhaps with a little lemon or lime juice.

feijão fradinho á la mostaza

black eyed peas are all over bahia (famously in acarajé) and frequently showed up at our table.

before adding the onions to your hot oil inject a heaping tablespoon of whole black or yellow mustard seeds. cover the lid in anticipation of savage popping and add the onions only when the music ceases. fry the onions closer to medium than high heat and add the garlic when translucent. add chopped tomato along with the beans, simmer in a little of the cooking liquid (as in the black beans, above), and stir more vigorously when the liquid vai embora.

we never had any in bahia but chopped mustard or collard greens would fit perfectly in this dish, in lieu of adding extra cooking liquid at the end.

feijão fradinho with *fenugreek and urucum*

another black eyed pea dish, this one comes out spicier and drier.

after the onions are brown add chopped garlic and green chile, brown for a minute, and add a toasted ground mixture of fenugreek and urucum. urucum, if you have it, is a red seed used mainly as a colorant in bahia. fenugreek is more commonly used in indian cooking and has an earthy, slightly bitter flavor. both are extremely hard and require soaking or toasting to be able to grind them properly.

continue as in the standard recipe, adding in farinha de mandioca or cornmeal in the end to cook for a few minutes and give a rougher texture.

green pinto bean tacos

i haven't seen them before or since, but green pinto beans refried with cumin and coriander made an excellent taco lunch one hot december day. i'm sure normal pinto beans would do the trick.

a slight unspoken glass of coconut milk gives the beans an added kick of creamy consistency.

serve with freshly ground roasted cumin on top.

1.3 mango salsa

- 3 ripe mangos
- 1 good white onion
- 1 bunch cilantro
- 6 malagueta chiles
- juice of 3 limes
- salt

the perfect salsa for a tropical climate, founded on the early 21st century mantra — "the mango is the new tomato". of course, in the old tropical world, the tomato was once the new mango. but never as good.

chop everything together. ingredients are listed in decreasing order of size. the bigger and sweeter your mangos are, the smaller and hotter your chiles should be. remember that lime juice and salt are your bridges and if something tastes wrong, you needs must build more bridges.

1.3.1 fruit salsa as a *pattern*

here the world is your oyster and no direction is advised. a good fruit salsa by my standards is sweet, hot, and sour. so take any fleshy fruit from peaches to papayas, add lime, onion, and chile, and you're on the road to success. some fruits go well with ginger, others with garlic, and many with nothing but pure hot chile peppers.

to experiment, walk around the grocery store or market with a chile in one hand and rub it over every fruit you see before taking a big slobbering bite. by the time you're evicted you should have a good idea of how to proceed.

1.3.2 variations on mango salsa

pineapple salsa

- 1 pineapple peeled and chopped
- 1 bunch of cilantro, stemmed and chopped
- 1 medium white onion, diced
- a small amount of ginger and chile pounded together

pineapple salad

pineapple is so damn good you don't actually need anything else. cube pineapple and mix it with salt and black pepper for a savory sweet spicy dinner salad salsa.

soy peach / papaya salsa

this salsa worked really well as a marinade one night when Wagner surprised us with an eel.

- 1 ripe papaya
- an inch of good ginger
- juice of two or three limes
- 1 tablespoon of honey
- soy sauce to taste
- cheap white wine to thin it out

the papaya should be ripe enough that cubing it leads to a small mess. mince the ginger, mix all the spices together well, and add the papaya gently so as not to purée it.

if you're from nowhere near the tropics, it's still important to look at this and make it your own. really ripe peaches are papayas in disguise and this recipe would be perfect for them, as well as overripe or poached asian pears and especially those overripe persimmons creatures (kaki in various languages) you can get on the cheap during the dying hours of the public market in the cours salaya.

1.4 standard brasilian table hot

so yes in this particular case 'hot' is a noun. you can (or at least, i could) go into any restaurant in bahia and ask "tem picante" (do you have hot?) to which the baiana would respond "teeemmmmm" (haaaaaaave) or maybe just bring you a little bowl of spicy vinegary salsa. depending on where you are eating you taste more chile or more vinegar. no matter where you are, asking for salsa is no good — they'll just bring you parsley.

- a cup of malagueta chile peppers

or any of their small spicy brethren. they're cheapest at the end of a market (get the ones that are going bad and pick through them, singing along to gilberto gil) or at a funny eastern grocery anytime.

- some under-ripe tomato

what we/they have in brasil; your standard supermarket hard-and-flavorless should do the trick

- an onion
- a few cloves of garlic

chop everything together into a small heterogeneous mixture. the peppers should be the smallest pieces and the largest total volume. add a little salt and pepper and cover with vinegar. let sit for a day or two, occasionally shaking. the infusion will of course get stronger and stronger as the days go on.

to use, you can either pour off the vinegar directly for salad dressings and medicinal purposes, or spoon out the mixture with its juices, like in brasil. always cover with vinegar after using to prevent the quick spoilage that is the specter haunting tropical lands.

1.4.1 the picante *pattern*

the simple idea here is that the material world is none other than your personal chalkboard, and you should look at gallon jugs of distilled vinegar in the same way a sculptor looks at driftwood or a child at construction paper. anything that tastes good by itself — and many things that don't, due to strength or edginess — will make vinegar taste great. and there's no reason to use flavorless industrial vinegar ever again, not when you have rosemary, garlic, dill, ginger, cucumber, or chile to spare.

the next time you're leaving the market with a measly two points in your pocket, you may happen to pass a tired farmer trying to reli(e)ve himself of a produce basket whose memebers have lost their virginal luster.

>	fear not. hesitate not.

clear him out, wash them well, add salt and pepper, and cover with vinegar for a whimsical while. you'll have pickled XXXX and tasty vinegar in a few weeks (or months) to validate your most minor of charities.

2.1 broiled zucchini steaks

- zucchini
- olive oil
- lime juice
- hot chiles (optional)
- freshly ground black peppercorns
- salt

vegetable steaks are simple, hearty, fast, and fulfilling. all you need is a broiler.

move a rack to the top of the oven and preheat the broiler. trim the ends of the zucchini (or whatever summer squash you might have) and slice it lengthwise into steaks slightly smaller than the thickness of your finger. the fatter they are the juicier and rawer they will be in the middle. marinate them in a baking dish or tray with the rest of the ingredients. in brasil, lime juice is easier to find than lemon — the key is to find an acidic taste to balance the oil. you can use vinegar too: balsamic and red wine both work great with squash.

clearly the longer they marinate the better (overnight would be divine) but i'm assuming we're dealing with time pressures and bad attitudes so it's generally good to start baking as soon as the oven is hot enough. it's not a big timecommitment to do a few minor preparations each night before going to bed — soaking beans, marinating vegetables, starting bread — but somehow those rituals have been excised from our cultural rituals and replaced by late night television. oh well.

place your zukes up close to the flame and broil them for a few minutes. the first black spots indicate they're ready to go — pay careful attention and flip them as they get to the level of charring you're comfortable with. the second side won't need as long, might be rather wet, and sometimes if they're thin enough i don't even flip them at all. move them to a plate where they can cool and await the sandwich of their dreams.

2.1.1 the lunch vegetable steak *pattern* explicated

the typical lunch/snack food in brasil, served at lanchonetes every twenty meters with tall glasses of freshly squeezed orange juice for less than 1 point, is a variation on the "X-Egg". X naturally is pronounced "cheese" and the "cheese-egg" is a fried egg and cheese sandwich on old white bread toasted with generous amounts of butter. high quality establishments, like our neighborhood joint 'parade obrigatória' serve it up with lettuce, tomato, and picante.

or those of you planning on traveling to brasil in this plane or the astral one, i may note that the "X-Egg" is something of an emergent property of language and cuisine, and neither the words "Cheese" nor "Egg" are necessarily intelligible on their own.

our complementary option was a vegetable sandwich with optional "X-Egg" on top of it.

as it was a popular paradigm at O Bigode, we came up with a number of variations. the markets usually had either eggplant, butternut squash, or zucchini, and the techniques would also work well with root vegetables. the variations we indulged in were of three types: choice of XXXX vegetable, cooking technique, and preparation.

the broiling zucchini number is fast and easy and works for most other vegetables as well. the fleshy ones provide the best results of course but slices of a large beet or rutabaga work great. starchy root vegetables (potato, yam, manioc) in a sandwich get a little on the chalky side for me and are best enjoyed on their own.

baking the vegetable, as is done in the squash recipe (below) takes a little longer and gives a sweeter softer taste. it's also appropriate if you want to throw a bunch of other flavors in with your main event: the added time helps them break the ice; the lower heat keeps smaller guys from burning as the larger ones finish cooking.

if you don't have an oven you can use a combination of dry roasting and steaming to get a similar effect on the stove top. lightly grease your pan or griddle, place a few steaks on medium heat, and cook until it starts to smoke and blister. flip the steaks, cooking another minute or two, and pour a small amount of water onto the pan. immediately cover as the water steams and it should cook into your steaks.

searing or breading the steak before baking it speeds up the cooking, adds another dimension of flavor, and provides an interesting texture. argentines and brasilians alike are fond of dunking food in egg and dredging it through flour before cooking, and the ubiquitous mandioca used in brasil adds a great crunch.

and yes, of course, eggs are neither considered vegetables nor vegetarian.

2.1.2 variations on broiled zucchini steaks

milanesa de berenjena with rosemary hummus and a gentle flower of baked garlic

slice your eggplant lengthwise as you did the squash, thinner than a finger in depth. many prefer the eggplant peeled but i'll leave it on if it's organic. nutrients and pesticides alike congregate in the piel, which often has a totally different (and usually more bitter) taste than the vegetable inside. if you don't believe me try eating just the peel of a grape and see what you think.

heat a pan on medium-high heat and prepare it with a little oil. if you happen to have any rosemary-infused oil lying around, use that. loosely beat together a couple of eggs (and maybe some water to thin) in a shallow plate and assemble the following in another one:

- 1 cup farinha de mandioca (or perhaps flour or cornmeal or any grainy grain product)
- 1 tsp salt
- 1 tsp freshly ground toasted cumin (or whatever cumin you have)

- $\frac{1}{4}$ tsp cayenne pepper (if you're up for it)

now take each steak, wet both sides in the egg-mixture, drip it over to the flour plate, dredge it, and toss it into your pan or grill. it will take a few minutes to cook each side — the batter will stick to the eggplant and brown — so the bigger the pan the faster this task will be.

as each steak finishes, move it to a greased baking sheet and bake as you would the zucchini above or squash below. while you're waiting for the eggplant to cook, take

1. an entire head of garlic and
2. cut off the tops (where they join together) and
3. rub with olive oil and
4. wrap in foil.

now put that present in the preheating oven while you're waiting for the steaks to finish. time it so that as the last eggplant finishes the oven is the right temperature for baking the tray. at this point the garlic should be half-way through its baking therapy and you can pull it out in a few minutes when the milanesas are cured.

as with the zucchini, you may need to fold or cut an individual steak to fit the sandwich, though some like the aesthetic of the hanging vegetable. butter the bread with rosemary hummus (see below) and place the entire baked flower on your lover or customer's plate. it's good for them.

squash sandwich with carrot mayonnaise and a tray of roasted vegetables

take onions and tranches of butternut squash and bake them in the oven with olive oil and black pepper and rosemary (if you brought it from argentina). when huenu and muticia handed you that bundle like a sword a season and climate ago, they knew, yes they must have known, but how could they have known where it would go and who it would be — that their commonplace mother of herbs would be *the* exotic touch in a land whose very name instills throes of exotic longing way down there in patagonia?

when they (the steaks, not your wistful longing — there is a word for that in portuguese — for lovers or lovers-who-should-have-been. at the time it may have made some difference but now the looks and the longing have settled together in a sweet smiling sorrow that helps with the illusion that yes you have lived) start to caramelize you can take them out. i like to leave the peel of the squash on but many humans are not used to such behavior. any other vegetables you throw in with the broilers can be put on the side. this is the steak of your sandwich

to doll up the orange meaty sweetness of the squash (or pumpkin or whatever is in the family at your local franchise organic farm store), i like to throw in a few cloves and ginger and sunflower oil instead of the above. the key magic ingredient to this — which being from a decidedly temperate fruit has neither right nor basis in an ostensibly brasilian cookbook – is quince. the perfume of the baking quince does a damn fine job of impregnating the squash. and you can use the baked fruit afterwards for any number of sweet or savory treats.

for condiments i would butter the bread with a version of carrot mayonnaise (see chapter five), and use thin slices of tomato and cucumber on top. alternatively, you could place the steak on a layer of torn spinach leaves (or other non-tasteless green, like mizuna, endive, or arugula)

and of course in traditional brasilian style, don't be afraid to toss an oily fried egg on top before closing that sandwich.

2.2   coconut sandwich loaves

- water
- flour: half whole wheat and half white
- coconut milk
- oil
- sugar
- salt
- yeast

if you know how to make bread, just make bread with coconut milk instead of butter or oil or milk or whatever you add to The Sponge to soften the dough. if you don't, know that:

1. bread is easy. bread is easy. bread is easy.
2. it was probably a product of laziness and sloppiness by some ancient man who couldn't follow his woman's instructions, which is to say, it's available to all of us and should be an integral part of our lives. if you eat gluten and all of that.
3. to make bread you need flour and water. that's all. to make tasty bread you also need salt. that's all. to make tasty bread and not have a live ETERNAL BREAD CREATURE living in your house day and night, you'll need to buy some domestic yeast.
4. there are exactly as many ways to make bread as there are names for the unnamable. don't let anyone tell you otherwise.

on the eve of each day we opened the restaurant, i would mix my yeasties in warm water with a few cups of flour. it formed a stringy paste somewhere between what you would use to flier a city and what your girlfriend's father might cook you for an awkward breakfast. then i would go to sleep or walk on the beach or listen to dj panozzo or have a few brasilian beers or whatever it was and in the morning the paste would have evolved into the beginnings of bread. this first, overnight, rise was considered so important to french bakers (back in the day, when people cared about themselves and the world that touched them) that selling bread that had NOT risen at least eight hours was a crime.

you will see bubbles of carbon dioxide throughout, feel powerful strands of gluten resisting your stirs, and smell the characteristic cheiro of yeasty living. this paste is called The Sponge. add half a can of coconut milk to The Sponge. at this point you may wonder, how much bread am i making anyways? well, you can always control that by the amount of liquid you initially add: XXXX cups makes XXXX loaves of bread.

after beating the leite de coco well into The Sponge, begin to add your flours. mix in each cup thoroughly and smoothly until you can no longer use a utensil. continue to add flour, cup by cup, until you have a smooth and slightly sticky ball, by Kneading together the dough with the raw animal power of your hands.

the goal of the Kneading is to lengthen and to harmonize the stringy tendons of the dough (called gluten) until you have a smooth rubbery live ball. a popular technique is to push into the dough (and away from your body) with the palm of your hand, stretching out the mass only to pick up the end and fold it back to where you started. as you begin to push again, turn the dough (or the entire bowl) ninety degree so your next push is perpendicular. if you continue in this fashion for 10 or 15 minutes your dough should be smooth, uniform, and symmetrically developed.

it is extremely important, across cultures and epochs, only to mix the dough with one hand. the ancients too understood that one must always keep a hand clean and dry to turn the bowl, answer the phone, etc. so much so that in argentina the expression for "getting caught red-handed" is "getting caught with your hands in the dough".

at this point the yeast need to frolic, yet again. protect the yeast by oiling the bowl (to prevent sticking) and covering with a damp cloth (to prevent drying). let them play until the bread has doubled in volume; the carbon-dioxide has filled the cubby-holes of the gluten lattice we constructed kneadingly. when the bread is large and incharge, uncover and take a deep whiff. making bread is a meditation and eventually we on this planet, together, will come to understand that the making is, itself, the true reward. press down upon the bread using your fist with a pressure correspondent to your mood. the spell is broken, the carbon-dioxide escapes, and you are left with the deflated doughy mess.

Knead again for a few minutes, oil gently and, cut the dough swiftly and surely into as many loaves as you want (remember, they will grow) and place in loaf pans to make sandwich bread. preheat the oven as your bread rises one final time. know that you are preparing for the wholesale slaughter of these creatures, for whom you have cared so deeply and so handily. and yet, somehow, this is not only okay, but as it should be.

when the oven is hot (say 350 F) enter the bread and do something else. be nearby and check them when you smell them, or be somewhere else and come back in 30-40 minutes. a few minutes after they look done, verify. remove from the pans and tap the bottom — a hollow sound indicates the flour has absorbed the excess water and the cooking is complete. turn off the oven and let the bread proudly rest on top of your stove. do not attempt to cut and eat them immediately as they will fall apart and burn your mouth.

2.2.1 a gentle pattern to breadmaking

there exist as many variations on bread as attempts to pronounce the unspeakable.

accepted ingredients

- flour

i would prefer to use finely ground unbleached organic whole wheat flour for one hundred percent of my baking needs. unfortunately, this bread often doesn't rise (most of the whole wheat flour you get isn't finely ground enough) to most people's satisfaction. and we've grown up in a white society in oh-so-many ways and maybe it's not even desirable to totally turn our back on the wonderbread fantasia of our collective past. so generally at O Bigode we used half/half whole wheat and white flour, trucking the whole wheat flour back from the store in Salvador and getting the ultra-refined/bleached/processed white flour from the mercadinho in Aratuba. in anglo-amerika, most co-ops have unrefined, unbleached, white flour which, while lacking the bran and germ of the wheat, doesn't include the chlorine and whatever other spooky chemicals people get to taste in their wedding cakes.

- water

any water that's healthy to drink is healthy for bread, and i would even use water that's not. you can boil water to stab out the impurities and use it for The Sponge as it cools down to warm. a popular measure for how hot is just right is the temperature your wrist can handle comfortably, without focusing your attention on trying to bend the Matrix.

remember that the amount of fluid in the bread (water + any fats or specialties you use) essentially controls the volume of bread you're making. the texture of the dough should be at least slightly sticky, and perhaps even wet. wetter doughs are difficult to work with and provide a moister final loaf.

- salt

salt, endorsed by french medieval bakers and neighborhood fatties alike, brings out the flavor of the bread and retards the rising time. it will kill the yeast if allowed to contact them directly (in the case of dry, packaged yeast), so make sure to mix them in solution. coarser salts tend to have more flavor and mineral nutrition — sea salt is nice, mountain salt is nicer.

- yeast

yeast are small fungi that are everywhere and alive. think of them as microscopic everpresent friends from the mushroom kingdom, sent to earth's airs to help humanity in nutrition and inebriation. we evolved together. the same yeast that works with us to make bread works with us to make alcohol. historically, humans picked up on the alcohol first, began cultivating grain (millet) to get more of it, and ended up with extra grain for less exciting culinary pursuits.

in the modern world it might help to think of yeast as alchemical machines transmuting simple sugars to carbon dioxide and alcohol. in baking bread we're mainly concerned with the rising power of the carbon dioxide; in making wine we're mainly concerned with the liberating power of the alcohol.

yeast are like volcanoes in many ways. as far as i have noticed, they exist among three main states of awareness — death, dormancy, and reproduction. they do not survive well in hot temperatures (hence canning and pasteurization) and are made sleepy by cold temperatures (so you can store them in the fridge). at room temperature and slightly above they are happy and active, reproducing early and often, giving off carbon dioxide and alcohol to their fungal hearts' content.

as with most things that are or were alive (like celery or chicken) one can choose to buy them (usually dead) or to care for them constantly and kill them ourselves. yeast are easier and cheaper to care for than chickens and if you're going to make bread on a regular basis it might behoove you to do so. all a yeast colony needs to live is sugar. this can be processed sugar, raw sugar, fruit sugar, or the sugar in flour.

how do i create and care for a yeast colony (already in progress)?

generally, selfishly, called a starter. that which starts your bread also, somehow, ends their blockparty. so be sure to give thanks.

mix a little yeast with warm water and flour and let it sit outside (temperate or tropical zones, dry skies) for a few hours. it should bubble and thicken. it is alive. store in your refrigerator to control population growth and take out a couple spoons each time you make bread. remember the words of meister eckhart "that which we take in through contemplation we must give out through love" — so be sure to

a) replace the colony you use with more yeast-food (some sugar, some flour)

b) share your holy bread with lovers and strangers alike. (some mornings this will be easy)

what if i don't have any yeast to start with?

you don't need to have yeast. the yeast have you. the sour smell of your garbage. the "rotting" pear at the bottom of your fruit bowl. the sediment in your microbrew. there are many more yeast than there are humans and they live in most places we do. to entice/trap some from the air simply leave some sugar/honey with water on the table for a day or two. cover with a cheesecloth or clean t-shirt to screen out flies and small children — the pores will be enough for invisible flying mushrooms to enter and to feast. when it starts to bubble, add some more sugar and flour to the mixture and, voila, you have your very own conspiratorial fungal colony.

what about other ingredients?

bread and beer purity laws, famous in france and germany, are the coy straitjackets of poetic form. like haikus and sonnets, they impose artificial limits in whose obedience we express ourselves and through whose transgression we taste novelty and freedom.

fats make your bread softer and spongier and should be used if you're trying to appeal to non-french or non-ascetics. traditional amerikan breads use milk, butter, or oil to soften their bread so it lasts longer before hardening and is easier to chew. because i was in brasil and i'm not particularly fond of milk anyhow i used mainly coconut milk for the fatty dimension. coconut palms are to brasil what cows are to india. and though the bread never tasted strongly of coconut, i felt good knowing it was there.

sugars quicken the rising time as they provide more food and easier access to the yeast. some of the sugar (from the flour and the sweetener) will not be metabolized and this residue serves to sweeten the bread. if you want your bread to taste store-bought, be sure to add lots of fat, salt, and sugar, as those are the stalwart roots of contemporary gastronomy.

eggs are amazing and there's whole books about them so all i can say is that if you're not opposed to it and you're using wheat flour, the egg will really help in the rising action of the bread. really, really help. beat it in to The Sponge with whatever else you're adding.

goodies and knickknacks. you can add anything you damn well please to bread during the final rise. sesame seeds, nuts, fried onions, bacon bits, cranberries, cinnamon, garlic, whatever. after you've punched down the bread and before you separate it into loaves (or after if you want some variety), take a handful of whatever you want to mix in and lay on your floured surface. knead the bread into and around your pile and eventually you will see little specks of pumpkin seeds or nutella or nori showing up all over your bread.

and if i live in a world with time constraints?

there are those of us yet uncomfortable with manipulating space-time, and it often happens that we decide we want bread in a couple of hours, not across the long night of our future. hell, there's no guarantee that either you or the sun will be here eight minutes from now, much less tomorrow.

so yes, you can make bread without letting it rise overnight. you can mix yeast and water in one bowl and flour and salt in another one. when both are uniform add the flour to the water and knead together until smooth. oil it well and let it rise in a warm place (maybe a preheated oven to very very low). let it double in size, punch it down, preheat the oven and let it rise again. when the oven is hot you can bake it.

or if you're really in a hurry, forget about the second rise, don't punch it down, and throw it (carefully) directly into the oven. you will notice the difference in the texture of the bread, but if you're hungry or craving in a profound way, you probably won't care.

2.2.2 variations on sandwich bread

cheddar / black pepper bread

1. make The Sponge
2. add butter and a cup of milk or yogurt, mix well
3. add a few tablespoons of freshly grated black pepper.
4. make The Knead
5. let rest, rise, and deflate
6. Knead in a cup of grated cheddar cheese and some whole peppercorns
7. form and bake

cranberry / walnut bread

1. make The Sponge
2. add 1 cup of orange juice, a few tablespoons of maple syrup, mix well
3. make The Knead, keeping it on the moister side
4. let rest, rise, and deflate
5. Knead in a cup of chopped walnuts and craisins
6. form and bake

savory breakfast bread

for eating with eggs, fried eggs.

1. make The Sponge
2. add olive oil, chopped sautéed garlic and/or scallions, raw minced chives, freshly ground black pepper
3. make The Knead
4. let rest, rise, and deflate
5. Knead with a little more olive oil
6. form and bake

2.3 brasilian hummus

- a lot of cooked chickpeas
- a few healthy dollops of tahini
- juice of a couple of passionfruits
- lime
- olive oil
- garlic
- roasted cumin seeds
- sal

our brasilian hummus was very similar to the traditional middle eastern variety. the only ingredients in the lebanese hummus we used to get were (in order of appearance)

- chick peas
- tahini
- lemon juice
- olive oil
- salt

to this i like to add freshly ground roasted cumin seeds and roasted garlic. since both are used extensively in bahian cuisine, they fit with the motif and appellation. the real new world twist however comes in the acid addition — limes instead of lemons (so much easier to find) and the alienheavenly bite of maracujá.

you'll probably never come across it unless you're buying food to make this recipe (why?) or find yourself between henry's tropics. but if you do, know that a good way to get the juice is to blend the pulp, seeds and all, with just enough (clean) water, and then strain through a tea or (more commonly available) juice strainer. the black bits will stay behind and you can use the (slightly) watered down suco de maracujá as your lemon juice.

the key takeaway of this particular slide is not "my food is so much cooler because it's tropical" or even that the taste walks you over to the sublime (already in progress) but that anywhere you go (more accurately, anywhere i've been) you can find the means to produce the flavor sense combinations that simple good food requires. hummus is about a creamy beany experience punctuated with yelps of citric acid. you can get that acidity from vinegar (ouch), raw mangos, sour oranges, gooseberries, grapefruit or even some types of jawbreakers.

2.3.1 varying the hummus *pattern*

as many intrepid cooks over the years have noticed, there are many types of beans and all of them seem to fit pretty well in the mortar, blender, robot, etc.

the basic technique i've evolved into using follows:

1. have your cooked beans ready to go. hopefully you pressure cooked and didn't hurt anybody (see chapter zero).
2. if you're using a blender or robot, blend the beans with a little bit of the cooking liquid in the machine. they should blend smoothly but not too watery.
3. when they've blended to just the right consistency, transfer to the mixing/serving dish and casually rinse the blender. since you didn't use any fiery spices or oils, it should easily rinse clear. this is important because blenders and robots can be a pain to clean if oily or left to crustify. also, with this technique you can quickly make three or four different "hummus" or "bean pâtés" in parallel.
4. add whatever spices, oils, vinegars, herbs, or vegetables you want and mix well.

some thoughts regarding flavor combination and proportion:

1. most hummus-type creations follow the model of bean / fat / acid / spices. beans are starchy and basic and will dry out (as well as ferment quicker) without the oily and acidic elements.
2. you often don't need very much oil, there's a wide variety of happy middle ground, and putting too much will make it taste disgusting. recipes will always call for olive oil and you don't have to use it. mostly people who cook real, good, food in the world can't afford olive and they do without. it's fine.
3. beans are large. don't be afraid to use strong spices in healthy amounts. garlic goes well with most beans. it's nice to use a fresh herb and dry spice in combination.

all of these spreads are good with any kind of bread product, though each has its traditional ally — hummus with pita, black beans with tortillas, canellini with toasted baguette slices.

2.3.2 variations on brasilian hummus

rosemary hummus

- chick peas (see chapter zero)
- tahini
- oil olive

- lemon juice
- garlic
- rosemary

this hummus variant uses an infused oil to incorporate the sweet strong flavor of rosemary into the dish. while the chickpeas are still cooking, place a couple cups of olive oil (or whatever oil you plan to use) on low heat at the back of the stove and drop in a few branches of rosemary. the oil will slowly heat and absorb the essence of rosemary. let them cook together for about an hour, remove the rosemary, and make the hummus as you normally would.

to give the garlic a subtler flavor add it to the infusing rosemary for the last 10-15 minutes of cooking, then remove and chop or blend as you would normally.

the herbal infusion can also be done without heating — simply cover a few branches of rosemary with olive oil in a bottle or jar and leave in the sun for a week or two. you can do this with any and every herb you find and build up an incredible collectors edition set of beautiful thriftstore bottles each with a colored infused oil or vinegar. you'll be the talk of the town.

before serving, garnish with a mixture of finely diced onion, tomato, and cooked rosemary leaves.

split pea pâté

- one or two finely chopped onions
- caraway
- cooked split peas (see chapter one)
- some vegetable oil
- fresh parsley
- lemon juice
- sal

this follows the typical model except the onions it incorporates are fried separately to give a deep taste and crispy texture. lay a pan on high heat, add enough oil to thinly cover its bottom, and add the onions when hot. you'll have to be attentive and stir constantly to fry well without burning. two onions will likely give you much more fried onion than you need but everyone loves fried onions so don't sweat it. when the onions are fully brown, turn off the heat, give a final couple of stirs, and incorporate into the pâté. if you prefer some spice, add cayenne pepper to the frying onions: late in the game but a few minutes before the end so their essence can mingle and develop.

the caraway seeds, toasted and ground, provide an earthy flavor that the beans desperately lack. if it ends up tasting like nothing, it's because there are too many peas for the onions and caraway. if you don't have caraway, use cumin, fenugreek, or even dill.

the parsley is finely chopped and gets folded in at the end with the salt and lemon juice.

black bean dip

black beans are generally acknowledged to be "the" favorite bean, so of course there are many ways to enjoy them. if you have leftover black bean soup or refried black beans, pounding or blending them into a dip is the natural next step in the evolution of your (you and the beans') relationship. unflavored black beans work as well but would benefit from the treatment given to the canellini beans, below.

- black beans (see chapter zero)
- some cooking oil
- garlic
- hot chiles
- ground roasted cumin
- raw chopped onion
- salt

it's generally more appealing with some whole beans intact, so i generally mash the pâté by hand instead of using the robot. the garlic and chile should be diced (or ground) together and mixed in from the beginning, so they have the most time to disperse. i add the onion last so it retains both shape and pungency. it's nice to serve a little chopped tomato and fragrant ground roasted cumin on top.

white canellini bean spread *aux herbes fraîches*

this spread differs from most others in that it requires a minor "refrying" of the beans to get the right consistency and flavor.

- garlic
- rosemary, lavender, oregano
- canellini beans (see chapter zero)
- salt
- black pepper
- olive oil

heat a couple of tablespoons of olive oil in a pan and sauté the garlic on medium heat. chop the herbs — use only what you have, every incarnation will be different and somehow equally part of the majesty of The Creation. when the garlic begins to brown and strongly flirt with fragrance, add the beans and herbs. stir and mash in a sweeping rounded motion until you have a white spread punctuated with bits of green and brown. some of the beans should be intact and provide a textural experience.

salt and pepper to taste; the final product should be creamy with a balance of olive oil, garlic, and rosemary.

2.4 a mediterranean salad, à la tropicale

the standard amerikan idea of "salad" involves lettuce, whereas i've found the typical other-world idea of "salad" involves any kind of random vegetable — often even cooked. culture from bulgaria to lebanon knows a salad heavily based on tomatoes, cucumbers, and some sort of feta cheese. feta cheese and good olives are available to the 1% of the brasilian population who know about their existence, dare to enter the upper-class supermarkets, and have the financial huskies to pull that sleigh. most of the time that wasn't our scene but in the final analysis, good olives are good olives.

- a couple of ripe red tomatoes, sliced radially into wedges and then again in half
- one cucumber, peeled, seeded, and roughly diced
- olives and their juice
- crumbled feta cheese
- $\frac{1}{2}$ a white onion, roughly but thinly sliced
- olive oil
- lemon juice
- salt
- freshly ground black pepper

i would cut the onion first and let it sit the lemon juice (we generally used lime) for as long as possible, to en-suave its sharp edges. failing lemon juice, wine vinegar works well. then i'd chop everything else and mix together. the olive oil is generally a strong presence, though not sickly dominant. as with most salads without crisp greens, this benefits from a few hours of togetherly marination.

2.4.1 Variations on longing for the mediterranean pattern

each micro-clime will have its own variations of course, but most seem to be based in tomato, cucumber, or both. the presence or absence of the local feta-type cheese is an important distinction, as well as the types of olives. fresh herbs, such as sage or thyme, add a nice dimension, as does minced garlic (either alone or with some olives, creating a partial tapenade vibe).

some cultures prefer to base the salad on chopped fragrant herbs such as parsley, cilantro, or mint. you can add equal parts of all three, finely or roughly chopped, to the standard version for a powerful and stimulating dish.

this whole school of salad can also be made with a cooled cooked grain as a primary ingredient. bulgur and couscous are used often in the middle east to provide starch, and texture. simply cook the grain as directed (see chapter six), cool, and mix in to the salad.

f you have easy access to it (like a tree in your back yard), avocado and coconut make great tropical additions to this salad family. i would toss avocado with a little lemon juice and add it at the end to avoid crumbling. fresh or dried coconut should be grated and toasted (very very carefully) and sprinkled on top.

2.4.2 variations on a mediterranean salad

lebanese fresh zaatar

- tomatoes
- cucumber
- olives
- onion
- lots of lemon juice
- lots of olive oil

and for the spices, equal quantities of:

- fresh thyme leaves
- sesame seeds
- ground sumac

couscous salad

- a couple cups of loose couscous, cooked in some coconut milk (see chapter six)
- diced cucumber or slightly underripe mango
- minced onion and garlic
- lime juice
- a pinch of cinnamon
- a handful of raisins
- carefully toasted pinenuts

tabbouleh

- a couple cups of cooked bulgur (see chapter six)
- finely chopped parsley and cilantro
- diced tomato and cucumber

- minced onion and garlic
- lemon juice
- olive oil
- salt
- freshly ground black pepper

serve yourself

in brasil and argentina, salad often meant a few distinct piles of vegetables on different parts of a large plate, include boiled potato and cauliflower, huge slices of underripe tomatoes, a small dish of olives, and some tasteless lettuce. let that be your inspiration

the plus side of the à la carte salad? it's a culinary structure designed to empower each diner to take control of her own gastronomic experience — we can all make our own mixture from the large-cut vegetables on a centralized plate. white wine vinegar, olive oil, and salt and in ready reach for each person to dress their own

refrain from mixing together:

- large tomato slices
- cucumber rounds
- diced sweet peppers
- onions in half moons
- a pile of crumbled feta

and a few doves, parsley- and olive-branches to decorate.

3.1 coconut polenta

- 1 packet or a few cups of polenta
- boiling water (more than 2:1)
- salt
- coconut: fresh, dry, or milk
- a lemongrass stalk or two
- some black pepper

boil the water. get a whisk or other implement with which you can stir with the steady vigorous focus of a true culinary Jedi. if you can find lemongrass, you can add it to the boiling water. the tea/soup this makes is excellent and vital for your continued survival on this disintegrating planet — MAKE SURE TO DRINK AT LEAST A LITTLE BIT. when the water is hot, turn down the heat to medium-low, remove some of it ($\frac{1}{3}$ perhaps) for "just in case you need more".

add your coconut product and mix before adding the polenta. if the coconut is dry (desiccated), allow it to rehydrate and soften for a couple of minutes before adding the corn. remember: polenta stands united and will clump together in culinary disobedience unless you (The Man) whisk down with surety and force. pour the polenta in a slow, steady stream, constantly stirring. when you achieve a smooth consistency, evaluate.

if it's looser/soupier than you like your porridge, lower the heat and continue to stir occasionally as you finish the rest of your preparations. in a few minutes it should thicken up nicely. if it's tighter than you like, add some of the reserved water or more coconut milk until you get Just The Right Thing.

do not take the polenta off the (low) heat until you are ready to serve — the texture and flow change completely as it cools. make it last and when your fools and lovers are ready to eat, stir in the freshly cracked black pepper and plate immediately.

3.1.1 the *pattern* amongst polenta's grains

polenta is (perfectly and paradoxically) both simple in its cooking and varied in its possible uses. the first incarnation of polenta is a sort of thick corn gruel obtained by stirring together ground corn with boiling water. this porridge can be cooked to a variety of consistencies and adapts to its form upon cooling, so it can easily be used for odd shapes or innovative presentation ideas.

for its initial cooking (described above) most people prepare polenta in one of three ways

- a loose gruelly porridge, with vegetables or spices mixed in or served on top
- a firmer more gelatinous porridge, served with an ice cream scooper and holding an attractive shape on the plate

- a focaccia-style creation, poured until flat and baked until firm

in the initial recipe, being a brasilian restaurant, i cooked the polenta with coconut and lemongrass. if you're not in brasil you probably won't (and shouldn't) follow suit because the coconuts, after such long and bumpy travels, will not be in a happy nutritious mood. other additions could be:

- chopped chipotle peppers and lime juice (the lime at the end)
- fresh mediterranean herbs (lavender, rosemary, sage, oregano, marjoram)
- chopped greens and garlic: beet greens, collard greens, mustard greens, chard
- milk instead of coconut milk, apples boiling in the water instead of lemongrass, and cheddar cheese with black pepper at the end

to achieve the second from the first merely continue cooking. as more water evaporates the porridge will become jello-like and hold together better. keep the polenta at a warm temperature (warm oven, warm water bath) until serving.

to achieve the third you can passively pour the hot polenta into a tray and let it cool, or bake the water out of the polenta in its new shape. i've found it easier simply to let it cool to room temperature and then even put the entire tray in the fridge for a couple of hours. make sure the tray has been lightly greased so it's easy (flip it over) to get the polenta out.

when you want to serve the formed polenta:

- remove it from the fridge, allowing it to return to room temperature
- cut it into whatever clever shape you desire
- sear it in oil or butter on the stove/grill, forming a tasty crust on each side.

3.1.2 variations on coconut polenta

lily's polenta breakfast

so there's this girl lily who lived with us for months and months and it's this whole other story but she dug the polenta and sometimes would have it for breakfast with nothing but some sugar or honey. however, if you live in the first world or are trying to impress somebody's parents you can put all kinds of breakfasty additions in your exotic corn porridge.

start by cooking the polenta (as above) and maybe using milk (if you're into that kind of thing) or coconut milk with your water. add sugar or maple syrup with the polenta and stir towards conformity. when it's ready open your pantry and inject whatever you like:

> raisins
>
> chopped dried fruit
>
> walnuts
>
> grapenuts
>
> toasted coconut
>
> picante
>
> yogurt
>
> granola

polenta with leftover sauté

this chapter's title dish takes freshly stirfried vegetables and mounds them atop a warm polenta porridge for a hearty, satisfying meal.

the next day you're going to have soft wilted vegetables and cold hard polenta sitting outside amidst empty beer bottles and scraps of purplecolor!purple ribbon on your floor. maybe some seashells and hemp bracelets in the corner and your roommates nowhere to be found. you're going to need some lunch before you can really focus on Ending Poverty or whatever else it is they happen to be selling on the culture channel.

- heat up a cup of water on the stove; add leftover polenta when hot, mix to the best of your ability.
- when more or less conformed, mix in a few chopped handfuls of last night's vegetables.
- while they heat together, dice a few green onions and juice a lime or lemon.
- take the pot off the heat, stir in some more black pepper, the scallions, and citric juice.

the fresh touches at the end (cilantro would also be nice) help one rediscover the vitality of the food. they are essential.

seared sun-dried tomato polenta

a more traditional polenta variation from our brothers on the mediterranean

- polenta
- water or stock
- sun-dried tomatoes
- white wine
- onions, diced

- garlic, minced
- basil, chopped
- cheese, grated

if your tomatoes are already wet and dripping with olive oil, chop them and you're ready for business. if they're still dry soak them for a few hours in white wine (if that's legal and desirable for you) or water. if you don't have a few hours, rehydrate them in hot water or wine for 15 minutes. when they're soft and wet, chop them and set aside.

heat a pot for the polenta with a little olive oil in the bottom. sauté your onions and garlic together on medium heat until they go from white to clear and feel soft and easy.

when the onions are translucent add your stock if you have some or salted water if you don't. when the water starts to boil, reduce the heat and add the polenta. if you forget to turn down the heat the polenta will boil over and you will have a hilarious mess. as the polenta cooks and smoothens, add the basil, cheese (parmigiano or romano if you're in the first world), and black pepper.

when The All is One pour into a tray or baking dish to cool (as directed above). let it relax to room temperature, chill in the fridge, and relax again to room temperature. while it's chilling you can press whatever you want into the top of it for fossilized spice or herb bits in your polenta. i use thin slices of garlic, whole rosemary branches, and tomato rounds.

when you're ready to serve, cut the polenta into pieces (squares, triangles, circles using a coffee cup, narrow rectangles to be seared on their sides) and perhaps in half heightwise if they're thick enough. heat some oil or butter in pan (good high heat) and reverently toss a peeled clove of garlic into the oil. when the oil is hot and garlic is fragrant, begin searing. each piece should cook for a minute or two on each side: enough to pop, brown, blister, and warm all the way through. it helps to cover the pan as you're searing the second side to add steaming action and make sure the middle is hot — especially for thick pieces. take care with slices who have cheese or fresh tomato on the outside edge — they will be blister faster, making them more and more attractive until they burn and are ruined (FOREVER).

cover attractively with sauce or sautéed vegetables and serve.

3.2 stirfry vegetables

nothing hits the Spot and the Complementary Contrast better for me than sizzling crunchy vegetables over a soft warm grain. you work for half the meal and are comforted by the other. take:

- onions
- green onions

- whatever vegetables they have at the market (carrot, cabbage, peppers, broccoli, cauliflower, beets, cucumbers, green tomatoes)
- garlic
- ginger

wash all your vegetables and peel the pestilential ones. cut them into thin longish slices that accentuate their shape and color. be adventuresome and don't worry about the forks of your fellow men and women. they will find a way.

heat some cooking oil (peanut oil, canola oil) in a pan, on high heat, and add the onions when hot. stir them well, constantly in motion: we want them soft and translucent, neither brown nor burnt.

while the onions cook, chop together a few cloves of garlic and pat's thumb of ginger. add the ginger and garlic when the onions are soft.

cook briefly and start adding the vegetables. hard items like carrots and beets should go in first, then cabbages, peppers, etc. spinach, greens, pineapple or other fleshies can go in last. the key is to cook everything exactly to the right texture so nothing is raw and nothing is mushy.

when everything is almost done, turn down the heat and add your sauce: either the peanut sauce (below) or any variation you see fit. mix together on low heat for a minute or two, until everything is cooked perfectly and has the right consistency, and serve immediately.

3.2.1 stirfrying vegetables following the pattern

if you're not going to eat your vegetables raw and really maximize the work they've done for you (and the work you have to do for them), then it's probably best to have them cooked as little as possible. stirfrying cooks vegetables at a high heat for a short amount of time, allowing sweetness to develop before the soggy sets in. it's work intensive in the sense that it requires a lot of chopping and a lot of attention, but these obligations are better seen as trainings — different yogas or meditations to help you relax into your true, eternal, selfhood.

1. wash, peel, and chop all your vegetables. take up a lot of room if you can.
    - it's easier and safer to chop vegetables with a flat side down. many vegetables are not born with a flat side and it is up to you to give them one. luckily, with a knife, this is not hard.
    - body- mind- and spirit- altering chemicals (nutrients, pesticides) congregate in the peel. you may want to remove it.
    - chop slowly and with dedication. relax. let it be a medication. having a bounty of vegetables around you is in itself a gift. having the opportunity to feed your fellow human is in itself a gift. if you focus on these presents you will grow full and fat before you have heated a single drop of oil.

2. appreciate them. the color, the size, the texture.
    - there are millions of US who do not eat when we want to.
    - there are millions of US who only eat the insides of cans and boxes. artificial colors and illusionary sizes.
    - you are truly blessed to be looking at a cutting board or countertop full of vegetables.
3. highly heat a small amount of oil in a large amount of pan.
    - use peanut, canola, mustard, or whatever the locals do.
    - olive oil and sesame oil will burn immediately, so if that's all you have skip down to dry-frying (below).
4. fry your onions first.
    - until translucent. onions take more stages of cooking to get to the taste and texture we want. so it's good to privilege them.
5. fry your garlic and ginger next.
    - just for a minute until they begin to release they're goodness. you don't have to use them either. you don't have to do anything you don't want to, regardless of what the police or your middle school teacher tried to tell you.
6. fry everything else in order of size and hardness.
    - this is the zen or dance of timing. it's very important and will take you a few tries it's worth it. there is an alternative (below) if you really think this desperate mix of on the fly density vs. surface area calculations is not for you.
    - good vegetables include:
        - carrots
        - xu-xu (see chapter five)
        - bell peppers of various colors
        - cabbage
        - cauliflower
        - broccoli
        - lotus root (if you're really living in style)
        - bok choi (or anything foreign that sounds like it's from a stirfry culture)
        - mushrooms
7. add your sauce.
    - some sauces (that have sugar or cornstarch or lots of liquid) like to be cooked to thicken and gloss. others want to stew to exchange flavors. and others just need to be mixed. generally the heat of the stirfry will be too hot for the sauce so you can either remove the pan from the heat or turn it down (or off).

that's just the standard way i've learned of cooking together different vegetables. there are a number of other easy techniques to get totally different flavors and textures out of the same vegetables:

dry-frying:

oil. if you're stranded on some lakeside in patagonia and don't have any or are prison to your ideological beliefs and can't find any organic non-gmo varieties at the local hypermarket, dry-frying is for you. it works best for a fajita-style mix of onions and peppers, but i've used it with great success on any vegetable that carries enough water to cook itself. as i understand it, the chemical premise is that the high heat steams out the internal water of your vegetables, cooking them from the inside-out as the hot metal sears them from the outside in. you should end up with some blistering and charring, to a degree you can control by how often and how vigorously you stir.

heat a pan to very hot. cheap aluminum or steel pans work the worst and will scar and burn easily. heavy steel pans, cast-iron and of course magical poisonous teflon work the best. throw in your vegetables all at once — onions and peppers or carrots or peppers and carrots or broccoli or carrots and beets or whatever. let them sit and cook at rest for a moment, and then begin to stir them. relax and let your intuition guide you — you will be drawn to stir or agitate that vegetable which is about to blacken until you are dancing with the heat of the pan, attuned to the microvariations of temperature, balancing the steaming and charring action. when the vegetables are appropriately soft, add roasted cumin, salt, or whatever other spices you desire. stir a few moments longer, and remove from the hot pan.

more authentically chinese stirfrying:

i've never done this but i feel i have to include it because it might be true. apparently stirfrys are traditionally made by frying each vegetable separately, then combining and heating the different elements together in the end. this technique is way beyond my levels of dedication and patience and i could only suggest it as a philosophical exercise, or for those who absolutely can't handle the idea of adding each vegetable to the mix at Just The Right Time to get the cooking to come out even.

gentler provençal-style sautés:

many cultures prefer to cook their vegetables on lower heat for a slower softer cooking. natural sweetness develops better, there is less chance of burning, and less work and attention required of the cook. follow the normal directions but keep the heat on medium, don't pay careful attention, and feel free to cover to encourage steaming (they're going to be soft anyhow).

3.2.2 varying stirfried vegetables

fajita style onions and peppers

follow the dry-fry technique from the beginning, using onion rings or half-rings and long strips of bell peppers. chile peppers work well too for a much more intense experiences. as they soften and start to blister i'll throw in a couple of chopped cloves of garlic to fry for a few minutes, as well as ground roasted cumin and a little oil (if i have some around). this cuts the burning and everything mixes together softly and easily. these vegetables are great in tacos, as a sidedish, appetizer, over polenta, or anywhere else.

instant sauerkraut

traditional sauerkraut is a conspiracy between various species of airborne bacteria and the human consumer, to preserve vegetables for months (or years) with added flavor and nutrition. this version replaces centuries of careful knowledge and technique with vinegar, which has a similar taste. using a flavored vinegar (see chapter two) would of course be preferable to the clinical distilled white you'd take home from The Store.

- as much cabbage as you can eat or chop
- some spices: dill seeds, caraway, black pepper, minced garlic, salt
- a sliced apple or two
- vinegar

use the standard technique for sautéing vegetables — medium heat in a little bit of oil, stirring enough so it doesn't stick or burn but not obsessing because the heat isn't quite dangerous enough. when all the water has been exorcised from the cabbage, add your spices and apples and cook together with the leaves for a couple of minutes. when the soft feels in danger of drying out, add enough vinegar to truck the cooking along. as the veggies steam more and the vinegar reduces, taste for acidity. it should taste sour and strong but not so much that you can't eat it. add more vinegar and cook until it's as strong as you like.

cover while people find the right chairs and wash their right hands.

onion, zucchini, and carrot taco filling

- diced onion
- half moon zucchini
- cubed or grated carrot
- cumin
- minced garlic

sauté these vegetables on medium-high heat, following the technique above which places the onions first and adds the zucchini and carrots when the former are soft. i add garlic and cumin to the onions a few minutes before the other vegetables, and squeeze on lemon juice and salt at the end. the zucchini have a higher water content and will finish softer than the carrots — the more you stir them, the saucier they will become.

sautéed potatoes

one of my favorite comforting weekend breakfast recipes, this sauté accepts a wide variety of seasoning combinations and can fill many roles on the p(a)late. the key is in the small and even sizing of the potatoes

- some potatoes cut into small frenchie cubes (brunoise)
- oil
- salt
- pepper

to make a brunoise cut, cut off a long side of the potato to give a flat surface. roll the potato onto this flatness (for security) and make a similar cut on the next side (for posterity). continue slicing down the potato, holding it together with your hand above the knife if it starts to fall apart. when you've sliced the potato into an array of thin (pinky thick) slices, turn the entire stack on its side (the second flat surface you created) and repeat the process. you will now have a matrix of matchsticks.

apply a ninety degree transform to your matrix and chop into cubes. the important part is to have a flat surface down at all times to allow yourself the peace of mind to make firm swift cuts without worrying about slippage and medical bills and your lack of insurance coverage.

heat more than enough oil to cover the bottom of the pan on medium heat. when loose and flowing, add the potatoes. they are full of starch (glue) and will want to stick to the pan, so it is your sacred duty to stir them often enough to prevent stickage. keep the heat on medium, cover the pan when not stirring, and cook for 10-15 minutes. they will eventually brown on all sides (if you're stirring evenly) and be cooked through (the smaller the faster). add salt and pepper, toss and stir a minute longer, and serve.

if you run into serious sticking problems, assuage the situation by adding a little more oil to the pan (not directly to a potato — he will greedily absorb it all leaving nothing for his brethren). adding water to the pan, which may at some points seem like a good idea, will likely cause over-steaming and a mushy potato result which you will have to rename before serving.

3.3 soy-ginger cabbage salad

one of the most popular dishes (among gringos) at O Bigode, this salad marinates thinly prepared vegetables with a powerful dressing.

- healthy cabbage
- bunch of carrots
- pair of beets
- green and white onion
- sesame seeds

- shred cabbage

- grate carrots and beets
- thinly slice white onion
- dice the green ones and toast the sesame seeds.

dressing:

- tamari
- tahini
- rice wine vinegar
- minced ginger
- minced garlic
- honey
- sesame oil

combine and mix vigorously. start with $\frac{1}{3}$ cup of tamari and $\frac{1}{4}$ cup of tahini; taste after each ingredient.

3.3.1 the *pattern* of this cabbage salad

three elements are key to this type of salad:

- vegetables cut with high Surface Area To Volume Ratio (SATVR)
- some time for the dressing to marinate and impregnate the high SATVR-cut vegetables (SATVRCV)
- a good dressing

within these constraints you can thinly slice (or grate; much easier with a grating robot) any vegetables together, let them soak with some good flavors, and enjoy.

3.3.2 variations on soy-ginger cabbage salad

a simpler teriyaki-style sauce

if the soy-tahini-ginger is a little much for you, this provides a simpler dressing or sauce for a vegetable stirfry

- orange juice
- soy sauce

- honey
- a little bit of minced ginger

mix the ingredients together until slightly viscous. if using for a stirfry sauce, be sure to cook a little bit on medium heat to thicken, and then toss in sesame seeds during the last minute or two of heat to speckle your vegetables.

asian dressed carrot apple salad

- carrots
- cucumbers
- apples

grate your carrots. if you are cooking for people who like vegetables and like asians, use 1 carrot per person. otherwise use $\frac{1}{2}$. always think about future versions of the self (lunch tomorrow) and any guests who might show up (doidão or elijah or otherwise).

mix the grated carrots with a liberal amount of rice wine vinegar. let them sit and negotiate while you finish grating.

peel and de-seed the cucumbers (using a spoon works dandy, just scrape down the line) and grate. use half the mass of cucumber as of carrots. squeeze them to remove the water (most of it) and reserve for a nice vodka cocktail.

peel and grate an apple or two as well.

drain the vinegar if you added too much, combine all the ingredients, and add the sauce:

- soy sauce
- toasted ground sesame seeds
- minced ginger

in general, the more sesame seeds the better, unless somebody is deathly allergic to sesame (ask).

apples in bahia?

every once in a while we would get apples. most crops grow year round in bahia but apples were cultivated in the south and harvested in the southern fall. so by october these apples had been in cold storage for six months and shipped from at least a 24 hour busride away. they were mediocre at best and cost over three times as much as mangoes.

clearly this dish would be hard to do without the carrots. everything else is negotiable. the combination i like is the sweetness of the carrots soaked in the sweet/tart of the vinegar. it's best with the rice wine (and indeed — just the carrots and vinegar is common in vietnamese food) but i've made it with just apple-cider vinegar as well. never saw a pear in brasil but little cubes of firm/crisp pear instead of apple would be perfect. you wouldn't even need the soy sauce.

3.4 peanut sauce

making a decent peanut sauce is incredibly easy, and making a great one takes about three tries. the key is to balance the creamyfatty taste of the peanuts (which we in amerika are very attracted to) with the flavorings that lend subtlety to the dish.

- water
- peanut butter
- soy sauce
- rice wine vinegar
- honey
- garlic
- ginger
- something hot

water your peanut butter down by whisking them together on low heat. take the sauce off of the heat and start added flavorings in the order listed. when it's salty enough stop with the soy; when it's sour enough stop with the vinegar. etc. trust yourself: if you like it so will everybody else.

3.4.1 peanut sauce *patterns*

i couldn't find anywhere else to put high-fat vegetable variations so here's where they're going to be. coconut, peanut, and avocado -based sauces are similar in that they start from a creamy fatty base and flavor it with the strong additions necessary to compete with so much luscious vegetable richness.

if you have access to peanuts or coconuts, THERE IS NO CONCIEVABLE NEED to buy peanut butter or coconut milk.

how to make peanut butter

take your roasted peanuts and put them in your robot. plug in and turn on. through the curtain of schrappy noise you will notice the peanuts go from whole to chopped to powdered to a big oily ball to a smooth creamy butter. after the ball relaxes into a butter, blend a little longer to force even more oil out of the nut. taste and add salt if you want "salted peanut butter". thin with water if you're making a peanut sauce there is absolutely no need to add oil.

how to make coconut milk

if using desiccated shredded coconut, soak in water for an hour and treat as fresh coconut.

if using fresh coconut, blend your coconut chunks in enough water to smoothen. this will take few minutes.

the smooth paste you get is coconut milk. what you find in the inside of an unripe coconut is coconut water. they are two different things. in the evolution of the holy coconut, actually, it is the coconut water that solidifies into the coconut meat, which dries into the flesh of the coconut fruit. to wit:

coconut water → wet meat → dry meat → grated coconut → coconut milk

3.4.2 variations on peanut sauce

coconut curry

a simple thai coconut sauce could be sautéing the following (as above) and letting the result simmer in coconut milk while you prepare everything else:

- onions
- garlic
- green chile
- ginger
- lemon grass

basil and cilantro in large quantities help turn the coconut milk green. this sauce then gets added to whatever vegetables you've just cooked, either merely to coat or as a sort of stew.

coconut chutney w/ mustard fenugreek

you can get a lot of insight into a culture from its markets and thriftstores. one device you could find in every kitchen/restaurant supply store in salvador looked like a horizontal orange juicer mounted on a hand crank (or electric), cost 40 points, and was used to grind out the meat of a coconut. so all you have to do is split it with your facão, drain the agua, mount it on the provided bracket, and crank until all the delicious meat piled up in front of you. definitely the way to go if you were making cocada or a lot of this chutney (say for a wedding) and were intent on using fresh coconut.

luckily, the recipe adapts well (as in, hell, everything adapts well if we adapt well, it doesn't have enough ego to care) to desiccated coconut: just transmute it into coconut milk (see above).

coconut milk (either newly made or purchased) is the base of the chutney. the other two components are fresh spices and roasted spices. for the fresh spices i use a mixture of minced ginger and green chiles, with more of the latter than the former. as for the dry spices:

heat a small amount of oil in a pan. when hot add 1 tbsp each of:

- black mustard seeds
- fenugreek seeds
- chana dal

they might be hard to find but here the flavor matters. dal just means split so i imagine you could break a couple of dried chickpeas and use that if you don't have chana dal in your house. chana dal is a really great lentil, however, and i recommend having it with you AT ALL TIMES. borders crossings and everything.

let the seeds pop and roast in the oil and take off the heat when browned. grind in a mortar and pestle until powdered. there will be some fragmentary chunks and that's fine. mix in the oil and spices to the milk, ginger, and chile. the chana flour you've made should act as a thickening agent, to help the sauce hold together. if it doesn't work, it's because you made the coconut milk too loose or didn't toast/grind enough chana dal.

it doesn't have to be very tight anyhow for dipping samosas or empanadas, but works great as a sandwich spread or on pita if it's a little thicker (like mayonnaise).

sweet and spicy aguacates

guacamole, while famous in mexico and everywhere else, is basically unheard of in brasil. they have many types of avocados, delicious and smooth, and never put them near garlic. instead they like their avocados sweet, with sugar or honey on bread, or in smoothies. so to be fair i'll put them both, though we made the guac a lot more often than the jam

guacamole:

- mix together roughly with a fork
- the lemon salt chile combination is really what's going to send you out there, and the rest of it is an important fashion accessory.

- a few soft, ripe, dark avocados
- half an onion diced small
- two minced cloves of garlic
- a little cayenne pepper

- juice of one lemon, maybe two
- a ripe tomato
- fresh ground toasted cumin
- salt

doce de abacate:

- mix together until creamy
- as sweet as you can take it (the brasilians take it pretty sweet) and the texture to spread on bread. add ice water for an interesting smoothie.

- a few soft, ripe, dark avocados
- a few tablespoons of sugar or honey
- a little bit of cream or coconut milk

4.1 chana masala

chana masala is a punjabi-style curry popular in restaurants all over north india and the west. it was the first dish my mother taught me to make and the most-requested item in my repertoire.

you will need

- cumin seeds and black mustard seeds

a good note on improvisation:

one general rule i cook by is that if i can't find the ingredient listed or don't want to be pushed into using it, i'll try to substitute naturally with something similar. often, especially with rare, expensive, or boogie items, it helps to arbitrarily strike words off of the ingredient until you find something usable.

for example if you don't have "black mustard seeds" try for just "mustard seeds". if you don't have "cumin seeds" you can try using just "cumin" or maybe some other "seed". what's the worst thing that could happen? ground cumin toasts quicker than whole cumin seed so you have to be more attentive. using another edible spice seed would give a different flavor and you'd end up with a different dish if you were to use anis or caraway. you might even win a fusion prize or something.

- $\frac{1}{3}$-$\frac{1}{2}$ as many chopped onions as cooked chickpeas, by volume.
- 1-2 cloves of garlic for each medium-sized onion, and equal amount of ginger and hot chiles
- cooked chickpeas
- a couple of tomatoes
- some chopped cilantro

and the following ratio of spices:

- 1 salt
- 1.5 coriander
- 1 cumin
- 1 garam masala
- $\frac{1}{4}$ turmeric
- $\frac{1}{2}$ cayenne

to make the curry, high heat enough oil in a pan to cover the bottom when hot. if you like that delicious fatty taste use ghee instead of oil and use twice as much as you really need. there's some truth to the argument, "hey, i'm vegetarian, i can eat as much fat as i goddamn please" unless you're talking to a vegan.

when the oil is hot, add the seeds and have a lid handy to cover. they will begin to pop fragrantly all over your kitchen. when you hear the popping stop, immediately toss in the onions. they should be chopped to a carpal's length. failing to do this immediately will result in the post-popping burning of your mustard seeds.

the onions are now frying in the infused oil, and you will agitate them vigorously until they brown. past sauté, past translucent, past browning, to brown. the color will actually change to brown. toss in the "wet spices": the ginger, garlic, and green chile you chopped together. fry together with the onions for a minute until they too have browned. the essence of the curry now awaits the dry spices, which provide both the musky depths of flavor and the signature color. sprinkle the mixture of spices (above, your homemade curry powder) over the frying onions and stir to incorporate. if you don't stir well they will burn before they brown — the key is to heat the spices enough to release their flavors into the oil and the air. as you continue to cook and stir the fragrance will continue to get stronger and the curry itself will start to stick.

persist.

only when it is sticking too much to stir add the chickpeas and lower the heat. if you do it too early the flavors will not have had time to develop and you will not be satisfied with the profits of your play. let the chickpeas visit and curry for a few minutes then add the chopped tomato.

my mother adds tomato paste and sugar as well, and her curry is certainly better than mine. we both serve it with cilantro.

4.1.1 the *pattern*: "how to curry anything you damn well please"

chana masala is an example of a "punjabi-style" curry made using onions as the vehicle to carry the flavor of dry spices through the curry. i'll outline below the general Form of all such curries. know that there are a variety of other forms, and you will not be able to make all curries with this Form, though the number of curries you can make is impossibly large.

1. heat your cooking oil (mustard traditionally, canola usually, peanut or soy if it's all you have). in brasil they sold non-gmo soybean oil at the local market and we would usually use that.

2. pop some spices in the oil to infuse it.

    black mustard seeds, cumin seeds, fenugreek seeds, and dried red chiles are all popular choices. mustard and red chile often go together.

    taking the curry in a sweeter direction, you can use a combination of cardamom pods, clove buds, cinnamon bark, and whole black peppercorns (this, roasted and ground together, is most of the mysterious garam masala).

3. after the seeds sizzle and pop, the flavored oil is ready to accept the main taste vehicle: onions

    dice onions evenly but not obsessively small. i use about half an onion per person i expect will be eating.

    stir the onions well at first, to coat thinly with oil and spices. fry past the soft translucent stage until they brown.

    the onions will turn brown and let the oil they've absorbed back out into the wild of the pan.

4. add your wet spices

    the wet spices, known alternately as "fresh" or "green" spices, are generally garlic, ginger, and green (or any color) hot chiles. depending on what you're going to curry, you will add somewhere between all and none of these. chop them well or mash them together in your mortar and fry for a couple of minutes before continuing.

5. add your dry spices

    dry spices are powdered versions of plant anatomy (flower, seed, bark, leaf, root) which lend an added culinary, medicinal, or aesthetic dimension to your dish. to capture a typical indian flavor you will use (among others) cumin, coriander, turmeric, cayenne pepper, cinnamon, clove, cardamom, white pepper, black pepper, sesame seed, asafetida, bay leaf, curry (neem) leaf, fenugreek, fenugreek leaf, and mango powder. there are age-old specifications of which combinations can be used with which vegetables, and i don't know anything about them. go with what tastes good and what makes your body feel good (from anticipation through digestion) and after much trial and error you'll probably arrive at the same conclusions the Ancients did.

    the key with cooking dry spices is to brown them enough to release their flavors. most spices you buy have traveled magnificent distances and have lost much of their potency along the way. any remaining umph can be released through heat — mix your spices together, sprinkle the mixture over your becoming-curry after the wet spices have been given a chance to brown, and stir constantly. they will threaten to burn and you WILL NOT BACK DOWN. continue to stir until you can smell every element of your spice mixture (even the salt, dammitt) in every corner of the house. only then may you go on. if you stop earlier you will end up with the grainy powdered taste of weakness instead of the full mystical flavors of The Orient.

6. add the protagonist, "she who must be curried"

    the curry is essentially ready at this point, missing only the object of her affection. at this point you can add any cooked bean (see chapter zero), leafy vegetable, cabbage-type vegetable, partially cooked tuber or root vegetable, or hard fruit. curries can be made of anything from spinach to mushroom to black-eye peas to apples. underripe mango. jerusalem artichoke. pumpkin. every piece of vegetative matter you find has a perfect curry waiting for it Out There in the noumenal realm — it is up to you to fish for it in the straits of possibility.

    lower the heat and cook the curry with the Object for at least five minutes. the Object needs to heat (and maybe cook), the flavors need to infuse, and you need some time to tidy up the kitchen. if you want a wetter, gravier curry, add a little water, tomato, stock, or oil.

7. finishing touches

after the curry has melded, adjust the salt. finishing touches are the spices that either don't need to or actively dislike being cooked: lemon juice, sugar, salt, cilantro. many heavily perfumed curries benefit from the lightness of lemon and cilantro; most gujarati cuisine adds sugar to balance the burn of spicy food. mix together your additions just before serving, taste, garnish, and send to the table.

4.1.2 a variation on chana masala

eggplant curry w/ brown rice

1. sauté onion on high heat in hot oil with mustard seeds and red chiles
2. add garlic
3. add cumin and coriander
4. add prepared eggplant
5. add diced tomato
6. garnish with cilantro

the variation inherent in this dish arises not out of its ingredients but its textures. which is to say, before recommending you start substituting celery for cumin and cucumber for tomato, there is a lot to be explored in how much you cook the onions and in what manner you prepare the eggplant.

to prepare the eggplant, salt circular cross-slices and lay them on a tray. yes, i know, you can do it in a bowl but must make sure that each layer gets access to the salt or it's all very well tossed together. the salt will draw (bitter) liquids out of the vegetable flesh, which must then be rinsed clean of impurities.

after perspiration and rinsing, bake the eggplant on an oiled pan. you can bake them until cooked through but still holding form, after which it's easy to cut circular slices into bite-sized sticks or chunks. or you can cook them longer to be mushier (making more of a uniform curry) or you can cook them shorter on a higher heat (closer to a broil) to end up with a more assertive eggplant identity in your dish.

similarly, you can caramelize the onions slowly on low heat, giving a sweet softness and soft sweetness to the dish. or you can fry the hell out of them with high heat and little oil, even blackening some edges and adding a mix of bitter crispness.

out of what has now been demonstrated to be a VIRTUALLY LIMITLESS field of possibility, i usually decided (was party to a decision?) on one of the following:

dry and spicy: this version has extra hot chiles, less oil in the beginning, sternly fried onions, lots of garlic, much more cumin than coriander, firm eggplant, less tomato. it gets a heavier cilantro garnish, an added dose of oil at the end, and not much in the way of a soupy-curry-tomato vibe.

sweet and easy: a mellow version with onions sautéed on medium-low heat just past translucency, moderate garlic and much more coriander than cumin, softer small chunks of eggplant (but still not mushy), liberal tomato influence and finely chopped cilantro mainly for visual interest.

of course, as always in life love and kitchen it is your sacred duty to TRUST and to FOLLOW whatever happens. if She calls while the eggplant is in the oven and you're over THERE anyhow trying to roll out tortillas with a soiled bottle of beaujolais nouveau, then you're going to have a smoother (not mushier but smoother) eggplant curry experience and you are going to love it.

maybe there's still some analysis remaining regarding the destiny of the future but the destiny of the past has long been clear to this side of the woodstove — everything She says and does to you happens for a reason, a perfect reason, and it's your sacred dharma to find out and to live whatever it may have been. we are given the spices and textures to create our own perfection if we can just muster the gumption to roll over and Do It.

at every stage of the dish, everything is possible. this is an especially beloved dish, probably because most people hate eggplant until they try it, and there is no zeal as fervent as a born-again berinjelador. there are only two ways to fuck it up:

- too much salt: if you didn't rinse the sweaty slices AND you added salt later on
- desire is the root of all suffering: if you cook the onions or eggplant differently than some idea you had in your mind, and then can't accept the consequences. the consequences are you altering the rest of your plan (for the dish, for the rest of your life) to take into account your new and wonderful reality, already in progress. if you hold on and fail to do so, that blockage, that resistance, that dissatisfaction will manifest itself on the roof of your friends' and lovers' mouths.

4.2 chapattis

chapatti is the standard hindi name for a north-indian flatbread. there are as many types of indian flatbreads as there are western risen breads, in a wide variety of shapes (circular, oval, triangular), sizes (thin and soft, thin and crispy, thick and soft, thick and heavy), and made from different grains (wheat, rye, millet, sorghum, lentil, rice, chickpea, and every combination implied).

to go into these variations is, as i have oft wanted to say, beyond the scope of this book. the simplest technique, to make the oldest bread product we've likely known, is as follows:

- flour
- water
- salt
- oil

mix your flour with a little salt and a little oil.

you can choose to add any (or no) spices as well to give your bread a little flavor on its own. most flatbreads are meant to accompany a yogurt or curry dish, and consequently don't spend much time developing an independent identity. traditional basic chapattis use "atta flour" which is either a mixture of wheat and white or a milling specification which produces a flour somewhere between what we know as "whole wheat" and "white". it is fine and unbleached. the small amount of oil mixed into the dough provides some pliability and mainly serves to keep each bread from sticking to the griddle with no added oil necessary.

take (slightly warm) water and mix it over and into the flour.

add water little by little, eventually forming a slightly sticky ball of dough. knead lightly for a few minutes but nothing considerable. the dough needs to rest for a few minutes and will soak up more water as it does so, so keep your ball slightly on the damp side.

when you have your rested ball, you should be able to push and to pull it, to tear off chunks and easily roll them into little balls of their own. rip off a couple for practice and place these little balls next to your mother lode. prepare your tools:

- a large flat area for rolling
- a bowl or shallow plate with flour
- a rolling pin or clean wine bottle
- a griddle or frypan on medium-high heat on the stove
- a plate to receive the finish product

you're going to spend exactly as much time rolling a little ball into a circle as it takes to cook a circle into a chapatti. in this manner as soon as one chapatti finishes cooking, you will be ready to place the next one on the grill. clearly you will experience much and terrible failure before you get the system down, but it's good to know: the first step depends upon the last.

to roll a ball into a circle, first flatten the ball into a disc between your palms. make sure everything is dusted with flour, including the wine bottle. roll out from the center of the disc away from you, and then switch directions, rolling towards yourself, passing the original center and flattening the side closer to you. as you continue the forward/backward motion, think of the wine bottle as a steering wheel of sorts, that is leaning right as it goes away from you and left when it comes back (or vise versa). in this way you are actually rolling a complete circle with each front-back motion. if you are using a moderate amount of pressure and everything is firm and well-floured, your circular movements should glide the chapatti itself into AUTOMATICALLY TURNING as you roll it, creating a perfect circle.

be patient. you may never see the famed AUTOMATIC TURNING. your friend may happen by and accomplish the spectral feat on his first try. do not take it personally nor as a judgment of your self-worth. we are all equal in the eyes of the stomach and every chapatti, no matter how misshapen or mangled, serves to pick up another bite of curry. it shall be in the end as it was in the beginning and there is only One Love.

to cook, toss the thin rolled circle onto the hot pan. make sure there's good light and watch the dough carefully. it will start to darken and to change its color. when the color has fully changed (maybe a minute) the underside has been cooked and the chapatti can be flipped. you will be able to tell which sections were thicker and thinner — the thin ones may be black or burned while the thick ones will have a paler raw color. as you roll better, the chapatti will cook evenly with no blowouts and no swamps. flip the flatbread and cook for another 20 seconds.

if you have a gas stove or an open fire, throw the chapatti directly over the open flame for a few seconds and watch it MAGICALLY INFLATE. it's a miracle and nobody will ever tell you how it works so don't bother asking. but it only happens if your karma is good and you were a focused chef. if not, it's still going to taste wonderful, you will make many friends and perhaps even influence some of them. try again in the dark hours of the night after sabotaging your smoke detectors and listening to bollywood soundtracks. all knowledge is memory, waiting hungover within you.

4.3 a brasilian cilantro peanut chutney

a big hit amongst humans, my mom taught me the antecedent to this recipe after much hesitation. it's a jedi mind fuck to equate its ease of preparation with the amazing swirl and fusion of flavor. take the following ingredients, roughly chop them until your blending agent can handle it (a bona fide food processor won't need any help), and put them in decreasing order of hardness. so, peanuts first.

- 200 g amendoim torrado
- 2 bunches of cilantro
- $\frac{1}{2}$ head alho
- 3 limoes
- 10 pimentas malaguetas

the peanuts should be roasted, the lower cilantro stems discarded, the garlic peeled, the limes juiced, and the chiles stemmed. at some point the blender might stop for lack of water. add coconut milk (watered down if the thought of XXXX grams of fat / mL doesn't appeal) until it blends well. salt and serve.

this is a very brasilian adaptation of an indian chutney that calls for twice as many fresh herbs and spices. you can pretty much add whatever you want, but the peanut / cilantro base is what unites us all.

4.3.1 the *pattern* drowning in the green stuff

the green stuff is always a big hit. the basic premise is that fresh herby leaves should be packed together for powerful flavor and possible preservation, though unless you seal a jar off, people will devour it all immediately. the green is often blended with strong spices like garlic or ginger and a source of fat and protein (some sort of nut).

for some plants, such as parsley, cilantro, arugula, or spinach, preparing the leaves is easy. you chop off most of the stemmy section and blend the rest in with the leaves without much worry. woodier herbs such as basil or mint offer the opportunity for more work and dedication — the best way i've found is to hold the branch by the head with one hand and run the other hand down the length of the stem, ripping off all leaves in your path. you're left with a naked stem and a crown of leaves which you can pop off in a simple motion and pick up the next branch.

nuts for green stuff recipes are generally toasted to bring out a deeper flavor, but can be raw as well (as in the typical indian cilantro-peanut affair). if you plan to make a lot, you'll be peeling a lot of ginger or garlic, and it helps to know the tricks:

- for garlic: to peel quickly, chop off the stem-side tip and flatten harshly with the side of a chef's knife (or a coffee cup). the skin should fall effortlessly off the crushed clove. if it doesn't, swear gently and crush again.
- for ginger: to minimize flesh loss while maximizing peeling speed, use the back of a spoon. it has just the right dullness to remove the peel without getting caught up in the meat.

robots are the preferred way of quickly preparing the green stuff. you can have a course out (pesto pasta) in as much time as it takes water to boil with a robot and a little experience.

4.3.2 variations on the green stuff

pesto

- basil
- garlic
- pinenuts
- hard cheese
- salt
- pepper

robot together, using olive oil liberally as a lubricant. i often use walnuts instead of pinenuts when i can find them on the forest floor, and tofu for parmigiano when cooking with vegan humans in mind. using a large amount of garlic and roasting it in olive oil ahead of time gives a deeper and suaver dimension to the pesto's bite.

salad green pesto

if you're lucky enough to get spinach, mizuna, arugula, or a similar green, and can't make salad out of all of it, throw them together for a great pesto. since they don't have as much history or fragrance as basil you'll need to have more spices or lower expectations of the flavor power.

- even mixture of mizuna and arugula
- even mixture of garlic and ginger
- as many walnuts as garlic and ginger walnuts
- half as much feta cheese as walnuts
- a little soy sauce
- a small green chile

cilantro peanut chutney with pineapple

another brasilian variation on the cilantro peanut chutney (the green sauce) popular with samosas; the tartness and fluidity here comes from fresh pineapple juice.

fresh pineapple juice is simply a pineapple in the blender and then through a strainer to separate the foam and any eyes you didn't properly exorcise.

i blend together the following:

- 1 bunch of cilantro
- 1 bunch of mint (just the leaves not the stems)
- $\frac{1}{2}$ cabeça de alho
- gengibre
- a handful of small hot chiles
- 200 g amendoim crudo

start with the peanuts to get a sort of crumbly peanut butter, add the sharp spices (garlic, ginger, chiles), and then the herbs. when it stops blending smoothly add $\frac{1}{4}$ of the pineapple juice and continue adding pineapple juice until the chutney is the right texture. you will have a lot of juice leftover and may want to convert some of your chutney into a marinade or dressing by thinning it further. or you could use the pineapple juice as the base for a new salad dressing. it will be so fresh and good that cooking it would be a goddamn shame and maybe you should just think no further and drink it. that's what we always did, anyhow.

4.4 gujarati carrot salad

i'm not actually sure if this is something i've ever eaten in somebody else's kitchen, but the pattern works in general. indian "salads" are often just one or two vegetables, grated or finely chopped, with a piquant oily dressing.

1. grate a bunch of carrots to an appropriately digestible size.
2. heat canola oil (mustard oil is better) on the stove, and when loose and easy, add turmeric and black (or yellow) mustard seeds.
3. you can add some grated ginger as well, if you're feeling in the mood.

soon the seeds will pop in the oil: cover or end up with some combination of sculpture and burns. when they finish popping, pour the oil and seed mixture over your carrots and mix well.

the salad is basically done — i sometimes add vinegar to help the carrots marinate. it's much better after sitting a few hours than right away.

4.4.1 a *pattern* for gujarati carrot salad

the idea here is just to make a spiced marinade on the stove and mix with a raw vegetable. you can do the above dressing (hot oil and mustard seeds) with cucumbers, onions, carrots, cabbage, or anything else you want. toasting coriander and cumin seeds provide another base. variations might include upping the amount of vinegar and mixing in a little sugar, taking the dressing in vietnamese direction.

4.4.2 variations on gujarati carrot salad

towards a carrot pickle

a variant of the carrot salad which people absolutely love is to throw the carrots into the oil instead of the oil into the carrots. this requires more oil, of course, which is why people love it. you can then add more spices, vinegar, and cook it all together until the carrots become tender. when you serve it change the label from salad to chutney and people will be psyched. however, you lose the raw fresh goodness of the vegetable. if you're concerned about that sort of thing.

- a lot of carrots, diced neatly
- equal and large quantities of oil and vinegar (enough to cover the carrots)
- ginger and garlic
- turmeric and coriander

heat the oil in a pan and add the spices (ginger, garlic, turmeric, coriander, and salt) when hot. let sizzle and cook until the ginger and garlic change color. add the carrots and vinegar and cook together until the carrots are tender. cool and baptize "quick carrot chutney". you can bottle and store or keep in the fridge — the oil off of the top will be great for salads and marinades.

5.1 black bean veggie burgers

so the burger has been long since liberated from pigs or any of that hambu(r)g (ding!) and once we see things As They Really Are, of course you could mash up anything under god's green sun, find a binder, and grill it. since i'm still abiding the illusion that protein Is and Is Needed by the body, O Bigode veggie burgers were always bean-based.

a veggie-burger being little more than ground up beans and spices, the key technical difficulty comes in forming the patties. if you and i are indeed the same person and you're hesitant to use eggs (out of ahimsa perhaps) or flour (because it sticks to your belly perhaps) to bind your burgers, you need to have the moisture content exactly right. too much or too little water and they won't hold together well or fall apart during cooking. again, anybody who gives you a recipe and tells you it's the Tao is leading you astray — there is only one unique moment for where you live and the humidity in the air and the temperament of your oven and how much water you really did cook out of those carrots.

- 1 lb dry black beans (should make a dozen burgers)
- one large onion, diced
- one large carrot, grated
- a few cloves of garlic
- a knob of ginger
- cumin
- oregano
- cayenne pepper
- salt

pcook the beans as directed (see chapter zero) and drain. if the beans are cooked too much and feel soggy it will be harder to form your patties.

sauté onions in a little oil with the spices above. fry them past translucent, releasing all their water and developing together with the cumin and oregano. you can either add the garlic and ginger now (to cook), or mix them in raw in the next step, depending on how strong you want their flavor.

when the onions are browned and fragrant, add the carrot and cook for a few minutes, expelling the carrot's pent up liquid and frustration. when your mixture is sufficiently dry, add it to the beans and mix well with your hand or a couple of forks. the starch from the beans should coat everything together and allow you to make individual patties. before starting, taste the mixture for salt and balance and make any final adjustments.

if you can't make patties which hold together well without sticking all over you and everything else, you may want to consider a binder. effective ingredients include:

- an egg, lightly beaten

- wheat flour, start with half a cup
- chickpea flour, start with half a cup

i usually used wheat flour, but not too much of it, if necessary. after making the patties and placing them on an oiled dish, i would chill the burgers for a few minutes in the fridge to help them hold together. chilling too much causes dryness and cracking, so, as in all things, strive for balance.

bake the burgers on a medium oven heat (say 350 F or 180 C) for fifteen minutes on one side, then flip and finish for ten on the other side. check frequently to make sure they aren't drying out too much — the surface should be firm and crispy but not cracking. since everything is already cooked, you're primarily concerned about heat, texture, and togetherness rather than whether or not it's raw in the middle.

black bean veggie burgers are best with fresh buns, fresh mayonnaise, crisp lettuce or spinach, and a juicy hunk of tomato.

5.1.1 the *pattern* to veggie burgers

so veggie burgers can be made out of any bean you have available, following the general process below

1. pcook and drain the beans
2. choose whatever vegetables you want to accompany them (onions, carrots, celery, leaks, squash) and sauté the ambient liquid away
3. elect any spices you might want (garlic, chiles, toasted cumin, herbs)
4. mix the beans, vegetables, and spices together at room temperature
5. form patties, place on a pan, and bake

the smaller the patties are in diameter, the easier formation will be. the thicker they are the better they will hold together and the harder they will be to eat. getting a wide thin patty (to resemble the frozen ones you've seen all your life) is the hardest because the beans and vegetables have no glue as strong as the meat product floating out there in the world. flour and/or egg make the binding a lot easier, and adding a little oil to the mixture helps as well.

5.1.2 variations on black bean veggie burgers

black-eyed fenugreek burgers

somewhere along the long and winding road i became obsessed with the combination of feijão fradinho and ground roasted fenugreek i had brought from india. for the first few months i couldn't figure out how to use the impossibly hard seeds and the only recipe i had for them involved sprouting. of course at some point she who discovered fire passed the secret on to me and i found that ground, roasted fenugreek had a rich, red, earthy, bitter taste that was perfect for one of bahia's favorite feijão.

- 1 lb dry black-eyed peas; soaked, pcooked and drained
- 1 tablespoon fenugreek seeds; roasted and ground
- 2 onions, diced and fried
- 1 bunch of green onions, diced
- a few cloves of garlic, minced into a paste
- salt

mix together, form patties, and place in dish coated with azeite-de-dendê. the dendê-fradinho combination is celebrated by baianos, and i trust them.

falafel

falafel is the middle-eastern veggie burger of choice. i've had it made from chickpeas, fava beans, and lentils, sometimes with bulgur and sometimes without. there are two ways to make it:

1. as above
    - use 3:1 ratio of chickpeas to bulgur (see chapter six)
    - mix in garlic, lemon peel, cumin, finely chopped onion
    - chop together a bunch each of cilantro and parsley
    - squeeze out the water (very important) with a towel and only then add to your sacred mixture.
2. as below
    - soak the chick peas overnight, rinse, drain, and blend thoroughly, adding water as needed for lubrication
    - mix in spices and cooked bulgur as above

after blending the chickpeas may need to strain out some more water, (use a t-shirt, cheesecloth, or pillowcase) if your robot isn't very professional. either way, falafel is generally made into smaller balls (closer to flattened ping-pong balls than burgers) and deep fried. eat it with hummus and tabbouleh and labneh in a pita. humdulillah

5.2 half wheat burger buns

making buns is essentially the same as making bread. i add more fat (leite de coco) for more sponginess, and make some obvious changes in the shaping stage. the buns will be smaller, rise more, and cook more quickly than your typical loaves.

use (unbleached) white flour for The Sponge and mix in

- vegetable oil
- a little honey
- sesame seeds
- sunflower seeds
- black pepper
- a little salt

the following morning.

when you tighten the dough up for The Kneading, start with wheat flour and gradually switch to adding both as the proportions even out. when you partition the dough for cooking, remember that each bun will lazily expand to fill any empty space in the pan so pack them tightly.

5.3 carrot mayo

- just enough cooked carrots
- 3-4 inches ginger
- soy sauce
- rice wine vinegar
- brown sugar
- cilantro garnish
- toasted ground sesame seeds

carrot dressing. carrot mayonnaise. carrot butter. carrot pâté. it's easy, versatile, and yet shockingly "original" to most of your friends' parents. if you want the taste to back up the color's promise, use carrots that DON'T taste like water.

the best cooking method is to sauté the carrots and ginger together in vegetable oil the thinner and more evenly you slice them, the quicker they will cook. use a medium high heat and stir frequently. as they get tender enough to mash or blend, throw in a tablespoon of brown sugar to provide a glaze. then blender them all save the two nicest-glazed slices, reserving for a garnish.

add small amounts of your liquids to help the carrots purée. i generally use a small amount of rice wine vinegar, more soy sauce, more sesame oil, and more water. when they blend easily add the ground sesame seeds and taste for sweetness and salt.

at this point ONLY YOU CAN DECIDE the consistency. for a mayonnaise-type sandwich spread, it's probably perfect as is. for use on a salad you'll want to dilute with salad oil and water to be able to

p
  o
    u
      r

5.3.1 carrot mayonnaise *pattern* speaks

the elemental idea of this pattern of sauces is that a smooth blend of a tasty vegetable with light seasoning makes an excellent condiment, running the gauntlet from marinade to dressing to salsa to mayonnaise to dip. it's the same idea as a pesto except utilizing the world of barely cooked vegetables instead of raw greens. you can make such a pâté from any vegetable you want. the only key is not to overcook the vegetable in question — after a few tries the spices will suggest themselves.

1. buy a vegetable you've never had before. peel it for good measure (how are you supposed to know?), chop it into bite-sized pieces, and steam it for five minutes. try a piece. if it tastes too hard, raw, or otherwise poisonous, continue steaming for another five minutes and try again. when you think the vegetable is ready for human consumption, drop a few specks of salt on a piece and try it. do you like it? yes, yes you do. fresh vegetables are good and salt is good and whenever the two meet, only goodness is to be met upon.

2. colocate the unknown steamed vegetable into the robot. process it, adding a little bit of oil if necessary for lubrication. if the vegetable has a strong flavor, use a mild oil (canola, peanut); if it has a mild flavor use olive or a smidgen of sesame. now add a little salt and taste it. what does it need? would it taste good with garlic? with lemon? with something toasted? with tomatoes? with raw onions? with caramelized onions? with orange juice? with apple juice?

3. open your fridge and assess its contents. look back and forth repeatedly between the mess in the coldbox and the paste on the counter. with whom would what jive? this shaking of the head is the essence of improvisation — a dance between getting what you've always wanted and getting rid of what you already have.

5.3.2 variations on carrot mayonnaise

beet mayo

- 2 large beets
- olive or salad oil
- 1 tsp ground cloves
- 1 cm ginger
- cilantro
- 1 lime

the technique here is basically identical to the carrot purée above. the spices are of course different, and i prefer the boiling method for the beets because of the nutritious tea / broth.

wash the beets well and peel if necessary (if they were venomously grown or have recalcitrant wa(n)ds of dirt). slice into chunky quarters and throw into a pot of boiling water. when they are tender enough to boil strain out of the pot and into the blender. SAVE THE WATER.

you can use the water for soup stock or to cook pasta, rice, or beans. you can drink it as a tea or chill it for an iced tea. it's very good and good for you. if you drink enough of it your pee will turn a reddish purplecolor!purple and really that's the best part.

blend the beets with enough of the reserved water to form a purée. remove from the blender (it rinses easily; water soluble!) and mix in some oil, the ground cloves, minced ginger, chopped cilantro, and lime juice.

you don't need a lot of beets to make a good amount of dressing. but as long as you're boiling beets, you might as well boil a few more to use chilled in salads later on. when the afternoon hits and you lose count of the beers, you can pull out a tray of cool vinegary beets and it will be goddamn perfect.

and a tip for boogie-impressive cooking: get beets of different colors (some purplecolor!purple, some golden, some chiogga) to make multiple versions of this and place side by side. they don't even have to be spiced differently — just put them on the same dish in yin-yang or checkerboard pattern and even the staid will cartwheel across your placemats.

5.4 vegetable ratatouille

we seldom had good eggplants at O Bigode and when we did i always made ratatouille. it's a tomato-based stew flavored with mediterranean herbs, popular in the south of france and generally served over couscous. i also like it as an appetizer with pita bread or chips and cold on sandwiches the next day.

- one large, bulbous, naked aubergine
- one long summer squash or courgette
- a few red and green bell peppers
- some onions
- lots of garlic
- oldish tomatoes, some cans of stewed tomatoes, or tomato sauce.
- herbes de provence (lavender, rosemary, sage, oregano, etc...)
- cayenne pepper or paprika

dice the eggplant into largish cubes and mix in a bowl with a few teaspoons of salt. set aside and do not disturb — the salt will wage war on the eggplant's hidden bitter juices, drawing them out of their caves to be rinsed away.

dice all your peppers and enough onions to have an equal quantity. cut the courgette into rounds or halfmoons. mince the garlic.

heat some olive oil in a pan and sauté as directed above (see chapter three). start with the onions and peppers, adding the garlic and red spice when translucent. after you add the garlic, rinse the eggplant and wring any remaining water out of the cubes. the salt has drawn the bitter spirits to the surface (in solution) and it's up to our heroes to vanquish them.

you'll finish as the garlic browns and all timing is perfect for you to add the courgette and aubergine. continue to sauté until all the vegetables are just soft, and as their released water steams away, add whatever combination of tomato essence (chopped real tomatoes, canned tomatoes, tomato sauce, ketchup) you have on hand. dump in whichever herbes you have, turn the heat to low, and let their power open up your mind. focus your mind, dilate your pupils, and notice your sauté evolving into a stew — the tomatoes' juices seep and comfort on every side, the bouqet des herbes slowly diffuses into every liquid corner, and the Many meld into the One.

you'll have to simmer for at least half an hour to thicken and cook out any acidic weirdness from the tomatoes and their cans. parsley and a considered teepee of finely grated hard cheese make a great garnish.

5.4.1 the *pattern* to vegetable ratatouille

ratatouille is basically a stew, and a stew — *selon moi* — is basically sautéed vegetables to whom are added liquid and more vegetables. ratatouille variations might hold the herbes de provence and tomato base constant while changing which vegetables comprise the bulk of the stew, which herbs are given more weight, and how spicy the end result is. besides tomato, coconut and peanut make good stewing mediums, as do starchy vegetables like potato or mandioca which naturally purée into the mix.

variations on herbes de provence

herbes de provence is a fragrant herb combo sold in cute yellow cloth bags in the south of france. it's a marked-up mixture of all the aromatic weeds native to provence, which might include thyme, marjoram, oregano, basil, summer savory, lavender, rosemary, sage, and occasionally fennel. if i don't have the name-brand variety i'll try to rob at least the sage, rosemary, and lavender from neighboring gardens, though the fennel adds a nice touch that can't easily be replicated (think pastis).

5.4.2 variations on vegetable ratatouille

west-african style peanut stew

sauté green peppers and onions first, like in ratatouille; add the following when translucent:

- a couple of small hot chiles
- a chunk of minced ginger
- SOME MYSTERY AFRICAN HERB

brown for a few minutes and add some sliced carrots (or other rooty veg) to the sauté. cook for a couple of minutes before adding a mixture of peanut butter, water, and chopped tomatoes (combined like in chapter three) to turn your sauté into a stew. turn the heat down to medium-low, cover, and simmer until everything is cooked through. if the soup is too watery, take off the lid to boil off some excess liquid.

salt and pepper to taste.

xu-xu moqueca

instead of the full-blown version (see chapter nine), sometimes i would throw together a quick xu-xu version to give foreign visitors a taste of this strange vegetable. it might be called prickly pear in english (or maybe that's something else) — a spiny light-green affair whose flesh inspires puffiness and a mild rash on those who dare to cut it. despite its ornery nature, i loved it steamed, sautéed, battered, and stewed.

if you can find it, be sure to peel the xu-xu well and remove the inner seed area. peeling it under running water helps with the rash as well but i strongly recommend getting the full-blown rash a couple of times for the experience. the puffy disconnection your hands undergo is not entirely unpleasant, and gives an immediate material reminder that we live in a complicated and dangerous wor(l)d.

if you don't happen to see it lurking nearby, any vegetable on the harder side (like a carrot or a potato) would work well in this recipe.

- a few xu-xu
- a large onion
- a few cloves of garlic
- a teaspoon or two of cumin
- two chopped tomatoes
- one can of coconut milk
- chopped parsley

real brasilian moqueca uses a special palm oil called 'dendê'. if you have it, use it and admire the deep red color and powerful fragrance. if you don't, any palm oil will have familial affinity, and if not, use peanut oil to get some sense of how fatty it should be.

sauté onion and garlic together on medium heat in your elected oil until translucent. add cumin and your thin spears of xu-xu (or whatever you chose for dinner) and stirfry for a few minutes. when the cumin's color and scent fill the kitchen, add tomato and coconut milk. stir well and lower the heat to medium-low — continue cooking until the vegetables are as you like them. salt and garnish liberally with chopped parsley. the color should be a deep oily red-orange with the dendê oil, and a pinker shade (somewhere between tomato and coconut) without.

5.5 standard amerikan condiments

ketchup, mustard, and mayonnaise. if you're living in brasil (and loving it) and yet need a nostalgic (the brasilians have a word for that) burger experience, you must synthesize amerikana out of (perhaps healthier) basic reagents. luckily for the culinary tripper, all three are a) pretty easy to make yourself, b) much better when so prepared.

ketchup

ketchup is an industrially produced reduction of rotting tomatoes with enough salt and sugar to disguise any real vegetative taste or texture. as such, a blender is helpful. take all the old tomatoes you can find or buy a few cans of tomatoes or unadulterated tomato sauce (in brasil, it's impossible to buy boxes/cans of tomatoes without sugar) and cook them over low heat for at least an hour on the stove. watch the volume reduce and thicken into a paste. when sufficiently thick add salt and sugar, stir for a few minutes, and transfer to the blender for final processing. start with a small amount of sugar, perhaps 5% by volume of the tomato sauce. continue to blend and taste until it begins to taste like "real" (fake) ketchup. stop when you reach your goal or are sickened by the quantity of sugar it involves.

if you want your ketchup to have some sort of flavor (maybe like barbecue sauce) you can roast the tomatoes beforehand and blend in roasted (or raw) garlic and onions. cumin too will make it taste more like adult food, but know that's against the basic premise.

mayonnaise

as far i can read on the label, typical mayonnaise has no relation to the traditional french process, which is fatty, delicious, and even slightly dangerous (oh my!) . french mayonnaise (called aioli when spiced up a little) is a carefully bound mixture of eggs, oil, and lemon juice. beat 1 egg for each cup of oil you're going to use and place in the jar of your blender. while running the machine on low speed, slowly drip in your cup of oil. if you drip it in slowly enough the oil will incorporate into the eggs in a beautiful demonstration of COSMIC UNITY and no separation will occur. add two tablespoons of lemon juice per oil-cup and continue with the oil, adding until your cup runneth empty or your mayonnaise has achieved the consistency you're looking for. salt. it'll be the best damn mayonnaise you've ever had and won't last long due to human and bacterial influences.

to make aioli, or its fancy (tarragon aioli, saffron aioli) counterparts, simply blend the eggs in the beginning with garlic and whatever herbs and spices you'd like to experience. use nicer oil. fresh herbs (chives, tarragon, parsley) work marvelously, especially the provençal collective (lavender, rosemary, sage, oregano). know you are a samurai and that most restaurant "aiolis" are made by blending food coloring with huge vats of jiggling hydrogenated mayonnaise.

mustard

mustard again is a simple construction made from vinegar and the mustard seed. the homemade variety i like gives an "old-world" style mustard that is nowhere near as creamy nor fluorescent as your standard variety. simply blend equal quantities by volume of mustard seeds and vinegar in a robot with salt, peppercorns, and whatever other spices come to mind. let it age a week or so to work over the bitterness and initial pungency into a suaver taste.

for 1 cup of mustard seeds and 1 cup of vinegar, you could also add:

- a whole head of garlic
- $\frac{3}{4}$ cup of honey (honey-mustard, anyone?)
- $\frac{1}{4}$ cup of horseradish

remember that you can use vinegar already infused (with garlic, herbs, ginger, whatever) to get a jump on flavoring your mustard.

6.1 stuffed green peppers with sweet potato dill filling

there are only so many curries you can do before the other beachfront hotels (new york apartments?) complain about the smell (goddamn immigrants taking over this county!) and it's no longer sexy to eat with your hands anyway.

though it's still more civilized. contrary to the idées reçues of the famously civilized occident, eating with your right hand and (but not while) wiping with your left necessarily presuppose a higher baseline standard of hygiene — your hands must be clean at all times in case eating or gnitae need to happen. from my brief sojourns There i got the sense that the average indian washed his hands almost fifty times a day.

carnaval week and all the country's transport had been appropriated for beer, so all i had for the crowds of brasilian vegetarians pounding on the blue metal doors fully three hours before the official meio dia opening were sweet potatoes — perhaps leftover from biriyani (see chapter 1) or barbecued out back by the goddess murals — and large green peppers, not too twisted and asking to be filled.

- one green bell pepper per human
- half as many sweet potatoes as humans (you'll have - leftovers, again)
- an onion for every three people
- ginger
- dill
- white wine if you're fancy, hedonistic, and not cooking for muslims
- suco de limão

making the filling

chop your onions medium and ginger small. sauté them together (in butter, why not, live a little, it's ultimately healthier to realize your temptations than to suppress them) on low, slow heat. instead of frying brown, they will cook slowly and sweeten, browning only after half an hour to show their true sugary nature. if you don't have a half-hour to burn, i would recommend reorganizing your life to demonstrate your commitment to personal fulfillment and the primary importance of food to your physical and emotional well-being.

short of that, when you get impatient, turn up the heat and add a little liquid (milk, water, wine) to steam out the rest of the rawness. when the liquid is gone, the onions will be ready.

add the dill first, cooking down and mixing well. when you see a good painting of green on white (my operational hypothesis: your tastebuds and eyes are so unified in their aesthetic sensibilities that the right color balance will perfectly indicate the optimal dill strength) add the sweet potatoes — they should already be boiled, steamed, baked, barbequed or otherwise wrangled from their natural state by the hands of men — to the onions and stir firmly, mixing the halves together (they were always destined to be one, *selon* aristophanes) in warmth and brotherhood.

you want the potatoes in small enough chunks to fit comfortably within a pepper, but not so puréed it looks recycled. it's going to be a little on the dry side and you can add lemon juice (not more than one lemon's worth) and any leftover white wine (according to the proclivities and majority status of your dinner guests) to the filling.

if it's still cloudy or taboo don't go another minute thinking that you can't or shouldn't add white wine or whatever alcohol you want really to any food at any stage in the cooking process. you can and should, subject to personal morality of course.

unless it's for a salad dressing most of the alcohol will cook off anyhow, but alcohol is particularly good

- as a soup stock
- in cooking risotto or rice in general (try $\frac{1}{2}$ cup of sake in your coconut rice)
- to marinate cabbage
- in pasta sauce (red wine works well here)
- for steaming vegetables
- for slowly cooking onions, leeks, shallots, or garlic

if your daddy's not palling around with H. McTyiere Smith III, you'll probably want to use cheap leftover white wine that's going to vinegar anyhow, and even then you'll seldom need more than a cup. if the wine is really hecho mierda just treat it like vinegar or even mix it in with one of your many flavored vinegar bottles.

making the peppers

as is generally the case, there is a traditional method used by indigen(i/o)us cultures with a deep appreciation of food complexity and lots of spare female labor time. also, you can boil them. if you choose the latter, just do so for a few minutes until they soften enough to be a little flexible. if you don't, you'll need live fire or a gas grill.

hold each pepper over the fire with tongs, chopsticks, or a couple of well-positioned forks. turn the pepper so the skin blackens evenly all around it. by the time the pepper is completely black it will be malleable enough to accept filling. now you just have to peel them.

let the two become one

with half-cooked empty peppers and a bowl of winey sweet-potato filling at your disposal, you're ready to start filling. preheat the oven, grease a tray, and decide whether you want the peppers to be top-stuffed or side-slit. the former involves pulling out the stem and seeds (perhaps with the help of a circular incision) and stuffing the pepper from above. for the latter technique, draw a slit down the pepper's thigh, allowing extraction of the seeds (shake it) and easier filling. this is usually an easier option, as the peppers will most likely be baking in a supine position.

most decadents — you've already used the butter and the wine, why balk at the label? — shine at the idea of adding cheese to the top of the filling and maybe over some of the pepper as well. as the peppers bake, the cheese will melt and the beginning of its browning will let you know Everything is Ready.

6.1.1 the stuffed vegetable *pattern* of culinary interaction

so,
    welcome.

welcome to the next level: stuffing. stuffing is an ancient and justifiably famous technique for either

a) developing innovative taste and texture combinations in the context of a microclimatic vegetable oven

b) hiding leftovers or otherwise under-desirables inside another vegetable, where it magically becomes "special"

as with all choices, the real answer is "neither" or "both". so, both.

like casseroles and lasagnas, which are beneath the scope of this book, it's a great way to recycle leftovers and keep the culinary excitement fresh. you can reheat virtually anything that was good yesterday, mix in something perky (finely diced onion, lemon juice, cilantro), and use as stuffing with a little parmesan cheese on top.

in brasil, besides peppers (see above) we often used tomatoes, which require careful excavation and no-baking. in addition to standard get-down-in-there stuffing, O Bigode — being situated a mere twenty feet from the historic colonial seaport of Aratuba — was no stranger to vegetative boats. the planet and i both like the 'nautical style' vegetable stuffing technique because it eliminates the need for flatware altogether. with a zucchini- or potato-boat the hungry customer sails away in a self-sufficient dining vessel, especially if they're comfortable wiping sans serviette.

preparation for hard-nosed tubers:

slice them in half, the long way, and boil or steam them until tender but not mushy — between ten and twenty minutes depending on your karma but in all cases less than if you were planning on mashing anything.

preparation for long squash:

slice them in half, the long way, tracing your fingers wistfully along any curves, and bake them until tender but not mushy. you want to be able to pick up the squash with The One hand and eat out of it with The Other.

if the flesh isn't fully done but it's getting too soft, just Pull Out anyhow and remember that the two most popular t-shirts in bahia were (no translation necessary):

> NO STRESS
>
> and
>
> 100% NEGRO

let the ministry be a blessing. which is to say, you can still scoop it out and finish cooking it later. and cooking is just indulging your lazy stomach enzymes anyhow.

for each vegetable you've built boats. eviscerate them (save the viscera) and gently massage the inside walls with assorted aspects of the Good: a little oil, a garlic clove, some salt, etc. then you can fill whatever suits your fancy (see any vegetable, bean, or grain recipe in this book) and bake to finish cooking. serve with a vegetable mayonnaise or other salsa, or atop a bed of grain (if you didn't use one inside).

the tomatoes are particularly great stuffed with something starchy — potato-pea curry or mujaddra have both been great. i like the potatoes more with onions and sautéed greens. everything seems to work well in the zucchini.

as with the peppers above, most humans are suckers for highly concentrated melted cow fat. and in the project of treating everybody with love, from yeast to the moon, there's sometimes some juggling. even if you're normally not part of a horrifically murderous system that wrenches breastmilk out of cows with cold metal tentacles, sometimes it's good to make a stranger (or amanda) smile.

6.1.2 variations on stuffed peppers

nutty zucchini boats

for this i proceed as noted above, mixing the following together for filling:

- feta cheese
- finely chopped nuts (walnuts or almonds, depending on climate and mood)
- brown rice (usually leftover)
- fried onions
- grated carrots or golden beets
- a little lemon juice or white wine

you can sauté the beets/carrots in ginger for a few minutes to soften or have them raw if you get off on that sort of thing.

a hint for proportions — if you have a large amount of brown rice, start mixing all the other ingredients together first and then add the rice so, while comprising the majority of the dish, it doesn't smother the taste and presence of all the fancy extras. if you only have a small amount leftover, start with the rice and add the extras accordingly, so they don't dominate and clash with each other.

crush the pepper over the top and bake until the zucchinis are ready to go.

baked guacamole

a pretty simple guacamole variation when you have the oven on and ready to go. cut open your avocados carefully, preserving both halves intact.

empty the avocado flesh into a bowl and mix in:

- one clove of garlic for each avocado pair
- a little lemon juice
- salt
- a very little cayenne pepper
- some bread crumbs, smashed up tortilla chips, or anything else crunchy and nutritionless
- $\frac{1}{2}$ of the cheese of you want to eat

fill the avocados once again with the mixture — the added ingredients should more than compensate for the pit's sudden lack, giving you heaping avocado experiences. top with the other half of the cheese you wanted to eat and broil until you get a nice fragrant croûte on top.

5.2 fragrant couscous with raisins and cashews

couscous, not a grain of its own, is a pasta made from semolina wheat, and popular throughout the middle east and north africa. it's a very small pasta and cooks almost instantaneously. i suspect that even very beginning meditators could cook it with their subtle vibrations.

the more traditional method is to pour boiling water over a bowl of couscous until the water level hits the couscous level (about equal quantities) and then cover immediately with a frisbee. mix in two bits of salt and olive oil into the 'scous before the water hits to keep it loose and evenly salted. after five minutes of steaming, you can remove the lid and fluff. it should be soft, light, and airy. most people add too much water and the scous comes out very dense. remember, you are both of the fire and of the air. honor that.

you can add other good stuff to the couscous before the boiling water or after cooking has completed. dry fruits (like raisins) will slightly rehydrate and become plump bursts of sweet awareness (generally a good thing). i like to add raisins and cashews, dried apricots and slivered almonds, or a small amount of ground turmeric and whole cloves.

another diamond technique is to use a perfumed oil (rosemary and clove come to mind) or sauté some spices in olive oil on low heat for a few minutes (as the water boils perhaps) and use that olive oil to mix in the 'scous before adding the water. i would do one stick of cinnamon and two cloves in this manner, and remove all plan(e)tary evidence before adding the oil.

6.2.1 *pattern* liner notes on cooking other grains

most grains we cooked were of two styles — rice and couscous. which is to say, they either require a lot of cooking (boiling, toasting, or baking) or just a little bit. when you're in a hurry or want to make a light meal, use the latter, which are generally smaller grains or products of larger grains.

of these, bulgur is the most popular and cooks just like couscous, except it takes 1.5 times its volume in water and wants fifteen minutes to cook.

when you have more time to cook and want a heartier grain, use whole wheat (not flour, the actual grains), barley, millet, or whatever else came out of the thresher. follow the instructions from the seller in terms of the water ratio and how much time to cook, but it's generally easy to check every ten minutes and see if your new rare and lovely grain is yet tender.

remember that it's all up to you, and you can use these grains in any of the above patterns, as well as develop your own ideas totally from scratch. from good ingredients and careful attention (a symptom of love), you can do no wrong. use bulgur as the object of your curries; use millet flour for half of your bread recipe; do fried rice with couscous. do it all. don't stop just keep going and know that every satisfied smile/belch combination is a small and pungent act towards a peace for the world's stomachs.

6.3 roasted orange tomato salsa

a lot of cooking is about color. this is a beautiful roasted tomato salsa that came out so nicely because the tomatoes were meio verde, meio madura, a vibrant orange that might mean "don't buy/use me yet" if had we other options. we had not.

roast them quickly by heating olive oil on medium heat in a wide pan while you chop the tomatoes in half. they all go in one layer nestled together until you can smell the black bottoms (maybe between 5 and 10 minutes). you can use fingers, tweezers or tongs to give them a flip and maybe a tad more olive oil, shake the pan and let them grill and blacken in a few minutes.

if you don't like the black bitter papery edges of the skins, you can take the blisters off. i think they have a nice color, taste, and texture, so i'll chop up the tomatoes skin and all. this is a good salsa for the blender but in doing so you denature the intangible quality hand-dicing affords. a 22nd century comprise is to blend $\frac{2}{3}$ of the tomatoes and carefully chop the remaining third (for texture, consistency, meditation) to add after blending.

dice the following to add to your roasted tomatoes, after blending:

- some onions ($\frac{1}{2}$ to $\frac{1}{3}$ as much as your tomatoes)
- a few cloves/head of garlic (to taste, roasted tomatoes hold their garlic well)
- ground roasted cumin
- $\frac{1}{2}$ bunch of chopped cilantro
- suco de 1-2 limão (depending on how sour those tomatoes were...)

salt to taste.

6.3.1 the roasted tomato salsa *pattern*

in the way that every man has his double and every puppet its shadow, every fresh salsa has its roasted analog. as most fresh salsas are based on tomatoes and chiles (of various species and colors), so too are most roasted ones. roasting gives a deeper, earthier flavor and can intensify the seasoning experience as well.

generally, when deciding to move a recipe from the fresh salsa pattern to the roasted one, the options emerge from deciding which elements will remain raw and which will be roasted. some roasted salsa are even reduced over the stove, unifying the flavors and cooking all of the constituents.

as always, experiment. anything you've done with fresh tomatoes or fresh chiles will be great with roasted tomatoes or roasted chiles. anything that comes from good ingredients will taste good in almost any form. we ourselves are the best instrument of our goals — if you seek love you must act with love, and through love; if we seek peace, we must create peace and be peace.

roasting chiles:

is easiest in a heavy pan on the stove. without oil place your chiles on the hot surface, turning when the chile blackens. many slice open the chile and vacate the seeds after roasting, but i like to leave them all in for sake the of father coffman and the rest of the world's sufi voyagers.

roasting sweet peppers:

is best in the oven. oil them well and slice in half. place on a baking sheet close to the broiler under the highest heat. cook for ten minutes or until most of the skins are black

— the waiting is difficult, but every minute you wait will save you five-fold in peeling. when blackened, remove the tray and let cool, covered with plastic wrap: the steam will help loosen the skin. when the peppers have cooled, you can peel away the charred black, revealing a pulsing red belly underneath. this is the meat to be eaten naked(ly), dunked in oil, puréed, or in any other joyful form.

roasting tomatoes:

generally as above. the greener they are the longer you'll want to roast them and the more you'll want the lid — so they steam more before total charring occurs.

roasting eggplant:

poke the eggplant in various places with a fork. cover with foil and bake for an hour (or until totally mushy) in the oven or, if you're near the flip side of a campfire, place the eggplant amongst the coals and leave it for a few campsongs. keep checking but the timing will vary greatly with the heat of the coals, but generally it will cook much quicker than in the oven.

let the roasted eggplant cool and cut in half. the pulp should easily scrape into whatever willing recipient you have. to get the true, smoky flavor that differentiates good roasted eggplant from bad, you must use a fireplace or buy large cans of 'mutabbel' from the arab supply store.

6.3.2 variations on the orange tomato salsa

roasted garlic tomato salsa

- heads of garlic
- tomatoes
- whole cumin seeds
- lime juice and salt

roast an entire head (or as many heads as you want) of garlic by cutting off the tips, massaging with olive oil, and wrapping in foil. place your package in the oven (best when something savory is already in there — not recommended to accompany apple pie or cocadas).

after half an hour check to see if it's soft and gooey. it should be easy to peel and eager to be blended. chop your roasted tomatoes by hand, mix with the garlic and some ground roasted cumin. taste before adding salt and lime.

roasted green tomato (tomatillo) salsa

tomatillos are a mexican tomato variant that grow with adorable husks and have a unique flavor. in brasil we used unripe red tomatoes which were, in fact, green, and pretended they were tomatillos. the salsa tasted great.

- roasted green tomatoes (or tomatillos)
- roasted green chile
- raw or roasted garlic
- cilantro
- lemon juice and salt

mix everything together in a mortar or blend in a few seconds with the robot. if you want it to be really fucking good, mix in half an avocado.

mahamra

popular in lebanon where they need more sweet than spicy.

blend with post-war consumption levels of good green olive oil:

- a base of roasted red bell peppers
- a few roasted red chile peppers
- a raw or roasted garlic (c/g)love
- lemon juice
- salt

babaganoush

also a middle-eastern favorite. as indicated above, the real roasted eggplant flavor only comes from the extremes of culinary presence — live fire or a lebanese can. your oven will not do the trick.

mix with a fork in a bowl large enough to handle some splashing:

- roasted eggplant innards
- tahini (a sizable but not dominant amount: keep tasting)
- finely chopped raw onion
- roasted garlic
- finely chopped tomato
- finely chopped parsley
- salt
- lemon juice (add last and make sure it's perfect)

when it's just right, add a few teaspoons of good olive oil, mix in, and throw another teaspoon on top. garnish with paprika.

7.1 introduction to empadas

the ⸤original economic thinking⸥ behind O Bigode was to make and to give freely all the food with cumin in the air, love in the heart, and no recommended price. the hope was to create an autonomous space for post-capitalist economic relations, where humans undertook commerce with gusto — not points or prestige — as their motivation.

barely a month after the grand opening, when the publicity machine was still getting started, Bigode collective members agreed to the first AEA (Amandan Economic Amendments) in an attempt to boost sales and to adjust to local cultural norms. The AEA included:

- adding fixed items to the menu with fixed prices, to be consumed at-the-bar or on-the-run
- expanding to include various juices in the lunch menu
- retaining the ⸤prato feito⸥ at no fixed price
- revamping the accounting system for both the culinary and alcohol divisions

the main result of the AEA was our decision to make two styles of veggie empadas everyday, with one of the fillings tame and one of the fillings exotic, to reach out towards the comforts and sensibilities of the island population. priced at merely a point and a half each, they were cheap enough that houseguests wouldn't think twice about buying half a dozen in a day, locals often got two or three, and even children would scrape together the resources to share one.

empada is the portuguese translation of "empanada", a savory fried or baked pastry popular all over latin america. we started each restaurant morning by making the dough for the covers (usually three dozen) and preparing the fillings while the dough rested. the oven preheated (and usually roasted vegetables for that day's salsa or vegetable main courses) while the bread rose and we filled the empadas. generally we would have finished most of the cleaning by the time the first round came out of the oven, a little before our noon opening.

how to make the covers:

we started out using a recipe dona victoria (of epuyen, chubut, argentina) had given me:

- 1 kilo de ⸤harina⸥
- 200 g de ⸤manteca⸥
- sal al gusto
- 600 mL de ⸤agua fria⸥

and after a few rounds amanda had it precisely at:

- $\frac{1}{2}$ kilo cheap brasilian white flour
- $\frac{1}{2}$ kilo expensive organic whole wheat flour
- 100 g of smelly unrefrigerated butter
- a seemingly equal volume of non-gmo soybean oil

seeming! seeming? out on thee seeming, i shall write against it!

- enough water to make a smooth dough.

you Knead the dough for a few minutes and let it rest for half an hour until it comes into its truly elastic nature. in the waiting period, you may perform whatever other duties call your attention in the kitchen, garden, bar, or dining space, but please remember the ants come fast for that strange smelly butter and your dough bowl had best be isolated from the counter by at least a couple degrees of separation.

i've weathered many arguments about ants in the kitchen, and ultimately stand firm in my belief that our relations must be co-operative. they communicate to us when we have cleaned well and when we have been lazy, they volunteer to cart away any last chunks of pineapple and cheese we missed, and they inspire us always to be attentive. in the kitchen's cleanest days the only ants to be seen were lazy scouts — the morning after a heavy debauch saw more wriggling bodies than counter space. the ants were a slow and deliberate mirror of our own community, of ourselves.

when the dough sighs with contentment and the fillings are ready and cooling, you may start the rolling. make sure everything — the surface, the rolling bin or wine bottle, your hands — wears a sportcoat of flour. check your rolling pin and surface for floury bumps from last time — they will cut your mambo like no other.

tear off a large jawbreaker of dough, flatten it into a disc with your capable hands, and place on the board. roll into a perfect circle. yes, yes, easier said than done. there should be some hints in the chapatti section (see chapter four). with the empanadas it's actually less important because a) no indian woman is going to laugh at you b) bilateral symmetry comes into play more than radial symmetry.

when you have a vaguely circular and strongly symmetric piece of dough, transfer it off your rolling area to a specially allocated filling plate. if it tears, it's too thin. place a heaping tablespoon of filling in the middle and give it the eye. you need to be able to fold one side of the cover over the filling and join it with the other side. know that it will stretch a little in the folding and place enough filling inside to be a competent snack. especially with vegetarian food, nobody wants to pay for something that doesn't really satisfy.

to join the two edges of dough together, rub a little water (it is glue) on one side. if your dough is wet, you won't need this, of course. then you have a number of options in terms of the repulgada, your first try should be with the fork: like a pie crust, use the tines of the fork to make consecutive impressions all around the joined halfmoon perimeter.

later you can actually try braiding — rather than look in a book or the mystical internet, i suggest you find an old argentine (or other latin american) woman and get her to show you. really, they're everywhere, one will surely manifest herself if you're attentive to the possibility. in a society whose primary social adhesive is alienation, a little old-fashioned intergenerational cooking is in itself an act of rebellion.

the empanada assembly process goes much faster with two people — one to roll and the other to fill-and-place. if Partner X is better she can also take care of other kitchen events (flipping the oven, turning down the pressure cooker, grinding the spices) while waiting for Partner Y.

place your folded emp onto a greased baking tray. bake the full tray for 10-15 minutes at medium (in brasil, i soon learned, they have no word for thermostat) heat, then flip all the emps and reinsert to finish evenly. another 5-10 minutes (they start to brown when done) until i-and-i will see them through.

alternately, you could deep fry them. yes, yes you could. another variation: beat an egg in a bowl and brush a little egg onto each emp before baking — it will give the finished product a professional sheen.

7.2 empanada fillings: butternut squash and madras potato

#1: *exotic butternut squash:*

- steamed or baked butternut squash
- an onion
- a few cloves
- ginger
- ground coriander

follow the curry pattern, flavoring the oil with the cloves and saving the chopped ginger (wet) and ground coriander (dry) for frying with the onions. when the onions and spices have browned together, add the chunks of squash (with a small amount of cooking water if available) and mix together. after five minutes of cooking the flavors should be well-acquainted: taste, salt, and taste again.

the filling, of course, should be moist but not runny.

#2: *madras potatoes*

madras potatoes are made using a different currying pattern entirely than the one presented earlier (see chapter four). no onions are used and instead the soon-to-be-curried maiden is dropped directly into the flavored oil.

1. fry mustard seeds and dried red chile in a little hot oil — just enough to cover the pan.
2. add 1 teaspoon or more of oil for each good-sized potato.
3. as the new oil heats add in a scant teaspoon of cumin for each person eating, and $\frac{1}{2}$ teaspoon of turmeric (total).
4. when the cumin has browned, add your potatoes in bite-sized chunks. be sure the oil is hot or the potatoes will suck up all the oil. you will need to stir attentively or otherwise discipline them into not sticking to the pan and burning.
5. continue to stir vigorously until the potatoes are cooked. you will have plenty of focused time to try stirring without a utensil (the flip method) or practice your portuguese. attend to other tasks at your peril.
6. when the potatoes are done, salt, garnish with cilantro and serve (or set aside for empadas).

7.2.1 variations on making empanadas:

almost every culture i've cooked in has a strongly rooted version of the empada pattern. india is famous for its samosas (deep fried tetrahedroids), el salvador for pupusas (stuffed corn tortillas), and italy for calzones (pizza folded in half). you can use the basic rolling technique above for flatbread or yeasted doughs, cutting or folding the circle to yield different shapes.

with respect to the inside of the equation, most of the rest of this cookbook is about making the fillings. the possibilities, i have tried to communicate, are literally endless. literally. not as in, "oh, yes mr. bigode there sure are a lot" but there actually is no end, no finitude, no opportunity to exhaust the different fillings that would be awesome and appreciated in an empanada. it's nice to have two or three on hand when making empanadas to appeal to different shades of the personality whole. we did a different style of braid for each kind so nobody gets confused.

rather than give recipes for each filling, i'll give a few and merely indicate the pattern and ingredients involved for the rest. consider it a test of sorts. empanadas involving corn, tomato, and potato were most popular in brasil, perhaps owing something to those vegetables' nativity to the americas.

tomato variations (generally with cheese):

- raw with garlic, basil, black peeper
- sautéed on low heat with italian seasonings (oregano, basil, rosemary)

- thrown in at the end of sautéing onions with italian seasonings

corn variations (the corn was canned with some sugar added. don't tell anybody):

- with garlic, spicy green chiles, and lime
- with garlic, salt, pepper, and cheese
- sautéed with translucent onions and italian seasonings
- sautéed with translucent onions and indian seasonings (cumin and coriander)

potato variations:

- cutely diced potatoes and carrots with cumin and oregano
- cutely diced potatoes with italian seasonings

bean variations:

- sautéed greens (kale, spinach) and garlic mixed with drained leftover black beans
- adzuki beans refried with grated carrot and ginger

vegetable variations:

- sautéed grated carrot and cabbage with soy, garlic, ginger, and sesame
- xu-xu tropeiro
- fried plantains with (a little) sugar, cinnamon, and hot green chile
- curried eggplant with lots of cumin and parsley
- sautéed onion and zucchini, reduced in beer

leftovers that might work well

- refried black beans and cheese
- feijão tropeiro
- roughly chopped fajita style vegetables
- drained ratatouille
- eggplant curry

7.3 pico de gallo

- 3:2 tomato to onion

- 1 bunch cebola verde
- garlic
- green chile
- salt
- ground roasted cumin
- cilantro
- lime
- a touch of cheap-ass sugary brasilian vinegar

chop and combine. chop and combine. chop and combine. (there are machines that do this — see chapter zero)

7.3.1 the fresh-cut salsa *PATTERN*

it's been generally recognized in the culinary world — except for an aberrant forty year period where microwaves were considered part of the communal future — that the best food comes from fresh ingredients and is chopped quite small. naturally, with these guidelines, you can't do better than a fresh, raw salsa.

what makes a good salsa really good is a synergy amongst its ingredients. as in a well-designed dinner party, each participant brings something different to the table — some of whom complement each other nicely, while others add unique and surprising elements.

in our poster child above, the tomato and onion form a polysensual frame for the remainder of the ingredients. the tomato is soft, red, and mild; the onion is crunchy, white, and sharp. the cilantro and green chile, both refreshing and green, serve to balance the suave and the pungent dimensions. the garlic adds gusto to onion's assault while contributing its own unmistakable flavor. lime and salt ground the salsa in their respective taste regions, giving the finished product a balance among salt, sour, and spicy.

finally, the fresh ground cumin adds a slightly sweet and slightly bitter earthy depth to the food that penetrates deeper and holds longer than the raw spices can manage. for the love oflove!for the love of krishna's bevy of virginal consorts, do not use old storebought ground cumin — it adds nothing but a stale dimension to your concoction.

to variate, think of replacing any of these elements with a similar substitute, or eliminating/adding balanced ingredient pairs. similarity usually falls into the following categories:

- by appearance — either vegetables which are the same color (when prepared) as whatever you're replacing or vegetables which are equally Not the color of whatever else is going in the dish

- by texture — ingredients that look and taste totally different may still serve the same crunch reflex for your mouth.

- by size — finely chopped or grated vegetables are easier to digest; a harder vegetable can replace a softer one if it is cut into smaller pieces.

- by taste — naturally, if one element satisfies the same taste region as another, it is a perfect candidate for substitution.

often a substitution will make sense within the framework of multiple categories. the key is to make sure you can justify the variation, either through the external imposition of arbitrary rules, a personal logic, or the courage of your whims. to taste excellent, a recipe (or combination) need only be inspired, considered, or tested — that is, have the blessing of Holiness, Deduction, or Experience.

some common examples:

- green or orange peppers can often be used instead of onion — they share the color of "not-tomato" and have crunchy texture. the flavor is of course totally different, usually on the sweet side, indicating one should add more garlic or chile to hold the pre-existing balance.

- onions, green onions, and shallots taste similarly enough to be used in each other's recipes with proportional recalibration. similarly with lemon juice, lime juice, and vinegar.

- chipotle peppers, red peppers, and tomatoes all share a red influence with widely different tastes and textures. their replacement signifies a major substitution (you will have a totally different salsa) but should always work well.

- fresh herbs vary totally in taste but offer a similar color, texture, and feeling of freshness to the dish. with the cilantro and parsley families, substitutions can be made with abandon, but branching out between basil, dill, mint, etc. generally require a deep recalibration of all the flavor attunements.

- one type of cooked bean (or corn) will usually have the same texture and acidity as another, leaving only color (and taste if it concerns you) to be considered when switching.

7.3.2   variations on pico de gallo

fresh chipotle salsa

- 1 can canned chipotle peppers in canned adobo sauce
- two hefty onions
- half a head of garlic
- a few limes and some salt

- diced bell pepper or corn (optional)

the chipotles are hot and this recipe calls for the whole thing just so you don't end up wasting any. it's generally best to use half in a strong chipotle salsa and use the rest with black beans or rice or in a soup or something large and diffusive.

chop the chipotles into a pasty mess and mix in your salsa bowl with evenly diced onions, minced or pounded garlic, the juice of a few limes, and corn or corn-sized pieces of sweet bell pepper, if using. salt to taste — the corn or peppers are mainly for visual stimulation and to help in the biomass effort to cut away the force of the chipotles.

beet apple salsa salad

- as much beet as apple
- a small amount of finely chopped onion
- ground cloves
- soy sauce
- grated ginger
- apple cider vinegar
- honey

in itself this recipe has four main versions, all of which taste different and are appropriate in different contexts purely as a function of chopping and texture. the main axis is of course the balance between the apple's light crispness and the dense, earthier sweetness of the beets. either can be diced (brunoise) or grated and mixing a grated One with a brunoise Other highlights the latter in a fine bed of the former.

for use more as a salad, grate neither; if your vision heads towards a dressing grate both. the border regions are the most interesting, of course. when you've found your balance, mix in a small amount of dressing, based equally in soy sauce and vinegar and modulated with honey in accordance with the sweetness of your produce. the ground cloves, if fresh, should be used sparingly and operate subtly, while the grated ginger heads the piquant direction and can be emphasized accordingly.

7.4 carrot hummus

carrot hummus is a cross between a typical middleeastern hummus and a carrot-based dressing you can pick up in new york or patagonia. it displays typical "hybrid vigor" for most crowds, has more cream and consistency than a straight-up carrot mayo, and more vibrancy and psychological nutrition than the standard (and much loved) hummus.

as with any hybrid, you can look it at from the perspective of either parent, generating two different recipes and tastes. i'll provide both approaches.

from the east:

- cooked drained chick peas (with some water reserved)
- cooked carrots (with some water reserved)
- tahini
- lemon juice
- olive oil
- garlic (raw or roasted)
- toasted ground cumin seeds
- salt
- parsley garnish

from the west:

- cooked carrots (with some water reserved)
- cooked drained chick peas (with some water reserved)
- rice wine vinegar
- sesame oil
- ginger
- toasted ground coriander
- salt
- cilantro garnish

a good place to start is to use equal quantities (masses or sizes) of the carrots and garbanzos beans. sometimes i'll serve this alongside a typical hummus, in which case i'll use a much higher proportion of carrots, with the garbanzos mainly for mass and creaminess. i've heard in some of the remote provinces it's fashionable to do the reverse — make a "flavored" hummus that has just enough carrot for a bit of color and sweetness.

i use garbanzos i've soaked and pcooked but of course the key thing is that you're eating, so if they come in a can, ultimately it's all sacred and nothing edible is to be disparaged. except the water from the can, which can be spat upon and discarded. the carrots can be cooked in any way that you like — boiling and steaming are the quickest, sautéing slightly longer but better flavor, and roasting the longest, but for me, the most rewarding. when i boil them i add ginger to the water from the onset, and save the stock against an arid day.

blend the two substances together. in a robot this should be fine. in a blender you will need some lube. this is a good time to add the sour (lemon juice or vinegar) and tahini (if you're rolling in from the east). if they still do not cream together, add some of the indicated oil or stock water.

with respect to proportions, it's easy to add too much vinegar and hard to add too much lemon. this is mainly because of the comparative work involved in squeezing a lemon and squeezing a bottle of vinegar. most recipes will call for XXXX tablespoons of lemon juice for XXXX cups of hummus. for most people it's hard to add too much oil, and if you're not one of those people, you would have gone with the water.

add the wet and dry spices (ginger or garlic, cumin or coriander, salt). these quantities are entirely to taste and there is much to be gained in their combinatorial experimentation.

capsaicin addicts can work in their cayenne fix at any time. when everything is mixed together, taste and see what should be lacking. you should encounter a good balance of acidity, piquancy, earthiness, and cream. the creaminess — provided by oil or tahini — is particularly important and DO NOT STOP ADJUSTING until you have it right.

7.4.1 *patterns* of salsic combination

thus far we've looked at a variety of salsa tropes: fruit salsa, chile vinegars, bean dips, fat (coconut and peanut) sauces, pestos, vegetable purées, roasted salsas, and the traditional fresh-cut variety. after a few grinds in the mortar and trips around the robot, it becomes pretty obvious these techniques can and should be mixed. indeed, people love the mix in flavor and texture that comes with throwing sautéed onions in a fresh salsa or roasted red peppers in a bean dip.

it's often easier to start with a smoother salsa pattern — the vegetable mayo, roasted veggies, or hummus for example — and work in fresh and chunky elements. for example, added chopped tomato or onion to a carrot mayonnaise brings you to a whole new level of fresh-salsa, building off of a creamy carrot base instead of straight tomatoes. inverting the notion of progress you could throw finely diced carrots and sharp spring onions into a smooth roasted tomato salsa for a similar textural effect.

another easier suite of variations is to mix two salsas together (the day after perhaps) in even proportions. i've found this works particularly well with mexican style salsa, fresh and roasted, based on tomatoes, sweet peppers, and chile peppers. half roasted-tomatillo (con palta) and half roasted-garlic chipotle makes a wicked empanada or enchilada sauce.

7.4.2 variations on carrot hummus

slippery green onion salsa

the difference between an easy-to-make salsa and a hard one, for me, can be seen in the soiled dishes, as wind in the waves of a lake. this salsa requires a lot of dishes. eventually you will mix the following four elements together

- 2 broiled red peppers
- 1 Tbsp ground toasted cumin seeds
- 1 bunch sautéed green onions

- a mixture of garlic, ginger, lime, cilantro, and chile

for the peppers:

these will take the longest and are the limiting step in terms of speed. first, turn on the broiler. split them in half, excavate the stem and seeds, and lightly oil. broil until the skins blister and turn black. it will take ten minutes or more — check back ritually after you do each of the following tasks. when they are black, turn off the oven, take them out and cover the tray with a plastic bag to hold steam in and loosen the skins. refrigeration also works well. go back to cooking. when everything else is done, they should be easy to handle. discard the skins and blend or mash the flesh into a purée. the smallest hint of vinegar can help.

for the cumin:

toast them without oil in a hot pan. when they darken, begin to smell absolutely fucking wonderful, and start to stick, move them to a mortar and pestle (or coffee grinder) to pulverize. you may use the same (hot) pan for the green onions.

for the green onions:

chop them finely and sauté over high heat in hot oil until they just begin to brown. do not let them brown further, but cut their mambo with some water. they will steam and hiss and come loose from the pan. when the hissing stops, reduce the heat and cover, they will steam to a tender slippery state.

for the raw power, dice or mortar together

- 3 garlic cloves,
- $\frac{1}{2}$ inch ginger,
- 1-2 fresh spicy chile
- the juice of 3 limes

keep a bunch of cilantro washed and well chopped. if you don't use it all now, you'll use it for something else. it's good for you.

combine the dry cumin, the onions, the purée, and the wet spices. salt. mix in enough cilantro so it gives a strong presence but does not overwhelm. the strong accents should be a power triangle of dry cumin, juicy sweet peppers, and sharp piquancy, with the tamed strength of the onions underlying it all.

roasted tomato black eye pea salsa

- olive oil and roast tomatoes
- blend them with black eye peas (2:1 tommy to pea)

- add in diced onions and garlic
- basil if you can get it
- fresh oregano or marjoram if you cant
- suco de limão

tomatoes and most other fruits and vegetables are best raw. but if you're taking this plunge and deciding to divest them of their unadulterated beauty, roasting is the way to go. especially for tomatoes and red bell peppers.

i have two methods of roasting tomatoes, depending on what else is going on in the kitchen.

stovetop: involves a heavy-bottomed pan on medium heat and tomatoes cut in half and rubbed with olive oil. when one side is black turn them over to cook the other side. this is easier in some way but steaming action happens as well and if you want the straight-up roasted flavor this is not for you. a plus is that you can empty the pan and it's hot and oily and ready to go for your eggplant or whatever else you have on the menu.

oven: tomatoes stemmed and rubbed with olive oil on an oiled pan under the broiler. they will black and blister quickly so be FOCUSED, AWARE and ATTENTIVE, which is really what the kitchen dance is all about anyway. so it works out. flip tomatoes when black the first time and remove when black the second time.

in either case, let them cool before you peel them and then throw them in a blender with some black-eyed peas. this recipe is perfect after you've made acarajé or refried black-eye peas or texas caviar and have a bunch of cooked black eyes left over in the geladeira.

remove the blend and add in the onions and garlic you chopped while the tomatoes were cooking. the onions should be diced small and the garlic minced. salt to taste and finally add the chopped basil and lime juice. lemon juice is probably even better but not so possible in brasil and really at some fundamental level of reality, past the artifice of "gourmet", "clash", and "palate" it's all the same damn thing anyway.

what we're doing with cooking — i think — is more than satisfying hunger or even artistic expression. i think we're cultivating a new type of human who will be the kernel of a new type of society. part of that human must be aware that food is not only nourishing and medicinal and good but also sacred, and he is a blessed being by getting to eat at all. that's why i think it's important to eat what's in season and to experiment playfully with limitations on your diet — the glory age of global gluttony might be fun (for some) while it lasts but pretty soon we might have to eat root vegetables and preserves all winter and it's going to be sad for the gourmands if they don't learn to love it.

that said, i do include a gourmet version of this recipe. in my experience, gourmet tends to indicate one of the following:

- spectacular nomenclature for decidedly unspectacular reality
- involvement of a strange animal product
- inclusion of expensive or exotic ingredient
- precise preparation required

since the first three options are philosophically unavailable to me, this type of gourmet involves concentration and a sharp knife.

before roasting the tomatoes, slice them into thin circles. place oiled cloves of garlic alongside them and watch them very carefully. cut the broiled circles into quarters and mix with very finely chopped onions. the garlic should be soft enough that chopping slides into mashing — mix them with the drained black-peas and lemon juice (not lime, jeeves, but lemon) and a few drops of balsamic vinegar (tell nobody and nobody will know) and add them to the becoming-salsa. rinse the basil leaves and stack them. roll from the tip end up to the base as if you were removing a carpet. then slice the curled leaf into thin wispy segments (chiffonade) to toss in lightly with the salsa. add the perfect amount of salt and serve with some whole roasted tomato circles on top.

8.1 texas caviar

i'd never heard of it before but apparently when matt came he made a large salad out of black-eyed peas and available delectables and this is what he called it —

- a pressure cooker full of black-eyed peas
  or
  the black-eyed peas you didn't use in your veggie burgers
- onion
- garlic
- cilantro
- tomato
- lemon
- black pepper
- salt

chop all the fresh and lovely spices together and mix with the black-eyed peas. there should be enough green, white, and red to create a sparkling taste sensation (other than the baseline beaniness) and maintain visual stimulation. the lemon juice plays the sorcerer, marinating the divergent elements together until they form a pungent and unified whole.

one
people
under
Management

as the old sages used to say.

8.1.1 easy *PATTERN* to follow with bean salad

so there is a Beauty and a Yoga to cooking too much so you have a creative amount of leftover raw materials to work with for tomorrow's lunch. i always make a full pcooker of beans even if i don't want so many veggie burgers or tacos, just to have extra around for Elijah or Experimentation. bean salads are satisfying in that the youthful vigor of their acidity and variety of spry ingredients often belie a powerful nutritional undercurrent. each bean is a unique and holy individual and must be spiced accordingly, but i've found stability in my desire for:

- chopped onions or green onions
- healthy dose of vinegar or lemon juice (the starch in the beans tends to get mushy and lean towards fermentation without a good Acid kick)
- leafy loving from a fresh herb like cilantro, parsley, basil, or mint

other spices — cumin, oregano, dill, soy sauce, ginger, garlic — vary from bean to bean. follow patterns and spice combinations from cooked dishes (with what do you refry them?) for inspiration.

8.1.2 a variation on texas caviar

garbanzo bean salad

- rinsed cooked garbanzo beans
  - celery
  - green bell peppers
  - large slices of tomato
- a few scallions
- some feta cheese
  - fresh dill
  - olive oil
  - tahini
  - lemon juice
  - black pepper
- salt

chop the celery and bell peppers together and mix with the tomato wedges, chopped dill and garbanzo beans. separately crumble the feta and mix gently with diced scallions. make a dressing of olive oil, a little tahini, lemon juice, and black pepper to pour over the bean mixture. top with the feta and green onions.

8.2 cold cream of beet adzuki soup

i know it sounds strange but it's awesome and the best color you could find. ever.

- a couple of beets
- a few cups of leftover adzuki beans
- soy sauce
- ginger
- tahini
- rice wine vinegar

- optional white wine
- optional coconut milk

1. chop your beets thinly and sauté them on medium heat with minced ginger. cook until tender, adding water or wine if necessary to prevent browning.
2. when tender, blend together until uniform and continue blending with a few tablespoons of tahini 3. when you taste a nice balance between the beets and tahini, blend in the adzuki beans.
3. continue blending, using the adzuki bean cooking water, white wine (one cup maximum), or coconut milk (no limit, soldiers) to thin to an appropriately soupy conclusion.
4. mix in soy sauce and rice wine vinegar, a little at a time, until the soup has the right amount of salt and sour. the tahini should manifest as a subtle background creaminess.
5. chill and serve garnished with mint leaves.

8.2.1 primordial soup *pattern*

it's chapter eight and if you're literate at all you must understand that COOKING IS SO EASY. you don't even have to do anything — some remote ancestral God and an army of Mexican farm workers have magically brought edible shapes to your kitchen and all you have to do is eat them. cooking at its most difficult involves splashing hot water and a dull knife. there's really nothing to it, and there's nothing to prove there's nothing to it like soup. the general idea is to cook whatever you have To Shit in hot water and salt. you can purée the result if you feel like using the words "consommé" or "bisque" but then you have to wash the robot. if you're feeling particularly lazy and don't even cut the potatoes more than once before dumping them in, label it "hearty" or "old-world".

i've often wrestled with myself in those pre-dawn post-enlightenment hours where the ghost of lucidity eludes me amongst pickle jars of cumin and urad dal — should i even write this chapter? what's the goddamn point if it's so self-evident. but, to quote robert hass, —

> After a while I understood that,
> talking this way, everything dissolves: justice,
> pine, hair, woman, you and I

— and everything we do in this beautiful human tragedy is so petty and obvious anyhow (and therein lies its majesty) that i damn well better write this chapter.

so, soup. we didn't make many soups in brasil because it was always so hot and everyone was high on fruit all the time anyhow. when we did they were either coconut milk stews (like moqueca), leftover bean affairs (see below), or cold and refreshing (see above).

most standard vegetarian soups start off like an innocuous stirfry and only continue to descend further into mediocrity. sautéed onions are met and cooked with peppers or perhaps carrots, water and other sundries are added, and the whole affair simmered on the back burner while the bread finishes baking and we, everconscious of our ant brethren, clean the kitchen.

as is generally the case, everything gets more interesting with a hit of cream, coconut milk, or puréed avocado at the end to bring a watery compote to thick and satisfying broth. cheese and bread-products (toast, croutons) also excel in this arena.

8.2.2 variations on the soup

vegetable black bean soup

pretend you are making a stirfry with onions, green peppers, and carrots. add the onions first and sauté until translucent. spice with garlic, cumin, oregano, and whatever else you've grown into doing as a chef. add the peppers and carrots and cook vigorously for a few moments.

at this point, a white elephant saunters into the room and reminds you that NO SIR you are actually making a soup. down goes the heat (medium-low) and in go the liquids — pcooked black beans, a few chopped tomatoes, some olive oil, salt, and extra water to boot. you stir and reduce for the better part of a liter of beer (por cozinheiro), check for thickness and life of the broth. if it tastes like water, add more salt and fresh herbs and continue to reduce. if it tastes like salty water, add more fresh herbs and some vegetable greens if you have them — or anything quick-cooking to flavor the broth.

please, for the One Love, do not use a processed cancer pill flavor cube to liven up your broth. suffer through our communal ignorance (remember dostoyevsky — we are each guilty for all), slurp your watery soup, and endeavor to do better next time. really. thank you.

a little cayenne pepper or crushed red pepper flakes makes the world go around with this one. i also like to serve it with raw diced onions, fresh ground toasted cumin, and grated cheese.

lily's thai soup

now lily is really beyond the scope of this book. i'll try to do some justice to her soup, if possible.

1. begin to stirfry whatever vegetables you have available.
2. manifest the soupiness

    (a) get a local brother to harvest some wild lemon grass
    (b) sauté (lots of) minced ginger and garlic and spicy hot chiles in oil
    (c) when brown, add water, lemon grass, and coconut milk

3. when the vegetables are almost done, let the two become one
4. adjust saltiness with soy sauce or fish sauce (go ahead. live with yourself)
5. when ready to serve add chopped cilantro and basil, simmer for a couple of minutes. and present with brio.

a simple gazpacho

gazpacho is ancient spanish for salad + liquid.

cut together, preserving the juices, of

- tomato
- green, red, bell, anaheim peppers (small pieces)
- cucumber (diced)
- onion (quarter moons)

salt the mixture to draw out the juices while you make a power pack of

- olive oil
- vinegar
- minced garlic
- lots of black pepper

tomatoes have a plurality, and it goes on down from there. both the oil and vinegar add strong and important elements — the vinegar particularly to marinate the soup together as it chills (at least a couple of hours). i like to add a cup of wine or vermouth as well, barring ramadan, to really get the party started.

serve with healthy amounts of chopped parsley or cilantro according to your clientele's neuroses and food allergies.

cold cream of carrot consommé

sauté your carrots, onion and ginger in butter. as the carrots finish cooking and gain a tender edge, mix in some brown sugar for a light glaze. cook a few minutes more and transfer to the robot. blend with a little soy sauce, vegetable stock, and whatever cream (dairy or coconut) floats your roots.

if by any stroke of cosmic luck you have fennel available, use it. you can use the chopped bulb instead of onions in the stir frying scene and a few sections of the leafy herb in with the soupy mass. taste the soup and water/coconut down to taste.

serve with gomasio (toasted sesame seeds and salt) in intricate and meaningful mandalas.

9.1 for those of you who...

a) no longer believe in coincidence

b) thought this might actually have some brasilian recipes

i've tried to collect some of the more popular bahian recipes for the Bigode community in a desperate quest for authenticity in a globalized culture. perhaps, through a few queijos quente tropicais, we'll all be brasilian one day: smiling, sexy, hungry, and 100% NEGRO.

cheese-egg

butter both halves of an old glutinous white sandwich bun or french roll grill or toast. do not clean grill beforehand.
while toasting, oil nearby grill real estate and fry an egg.
as the egg solidifies, lay a slab of yellowish cheese atop it.
the cheese melts as the egg finishes.

impurists have the option of searching out a few slices of underripe tomato and yesterday's lettuce.

bread → lettuce → tomato → egg → cheese → bread

queijo quente tropical

the brasilian version of yesterday's grilled-cheese sandwich, which amanda discovered on the menu of one of our staple internet cafes. it had always been there i guess, as old as pineapples and slavery, cleverly hidden amongst wicker chairs, 500 mL bowls of açaí com banana, and the most amazing book i've been blessed by browsing: frutas do brasil

use three thin pieces of white (or white/wheat) bread,
grill cheese slices between slices one and two,
pineapple slices between slices two and three.
assemble with lettuce and tomato

acarajé

the premier bahian snack food, a large deep-fried falafel-esque creature made from black-eyed peas that originated as a sacrament for candomblé rituals.

soak "feijão fradinho quebrado" (broken black-eye peas) over night. if you can't find the broken ones, briefly blend whole ones until they break. rinse and drain the beans, soak again, and rinse again. continue every couple of hours until you've rinsed away all the hulls, until you see just the whiteness of the beans.

robot the soaked, rinsed, drained, hulled beans with an onion. add small amounts of water to facilitate a smooth blending. you will end up with a foamy pancakey dough. let the dough rise for a few hours (in brasil) or a day in a preheated oven (in wintry temperate climes). it will ferment and conspire with yeast in the air to bulk up and gain a sour edge.

stir the dough, form with your hand into firm patties the diameter of cheap hamburgers and much thicker. deep fry in hot oil — the baianos use the wonderfully fragrant and fattening azeite-de-dendê. it's red and cooks the acarajé a deep reddish brown.

to serve, hot!, the brasilians slice down the center and add some of the following:

- vatapá: coconut shrimp paste
- caruru: slimy curried okra
- pimenta: spicy chile sauce
- salada: unripe tomatoes and onions

i never got close enough to a proper baiana to learn how to make them. they're sacred anyhow and probably best left to the priestesses and professionals.

peixe frito

every restaurant in brasil had one thing, fish, cooked in two ways: frito and moqueca. it always came with rice and beans and salad (tomatoes and onions) and hot sauce and of course lots of beer. and it was truly excellent. all of the restaurants were on the beach and the women would cook what the men had brought in from the sea that morning — usually peixe vermelho.

clearly this isn't a vegetarian recipe, but it's not much of a recipe anyhow, so i'm not sweating it either.

1. go outside and catch a red fish (peixe vermelho)
2. clean it with a sharp tetanic looking knife and when the customers order
3. marinate it for 15 minutes in garlic, onion, salt, and lemon juice.
4. after they've had a few rounds of beer, gently place the entire fish in a vat of hot oil and fry it until done
5. the flesh will move away from the bone as the skin crispens. it's done.
6. serve on a bed of lettuce with steaming bowls of pinto beans and rice, and another round of beer.

feijão tropeiro

feijão tropeiro, as i understand it, is a dish from the south of brasil (perhaps minas gerais) where the familiar black-eyed pea is sautéed with spices and dusted heavily with the ubiquitous farinha de mandioca, so it gets a dry, grainy texture. it's good if you have plenty of beer on hand to wash it down. luckily, brasilians always do.

sauté diced onion, diced tomato, a little garlic all together in a little cooking oil. when the onions have mostly cooked and the tomatoes are pretty dry, add the black-eye peas and cook together. when the onions are fully done the flavors will have unified (UNITY!) and you can squeeze in some lime juice and dump in a good amount of farinha. keep stirring and adding farinha until the beans are well-bespeckled and you get that dry, chalky feeling just looking at it.

salt and serve with coentro picado.

moqueca

moqueca is bahia's most famous dish, a fish stew simmered in azeite-de-dendê, leite de coco, e tomate. i documented how to make it before even making it to bahia, from a kind restaurateur in paraty (near rio de janeiro).

fernando says, serve de 2 a 3 pessoas:

1. heat a clay pot with tall fire for at least ten minutes
2. locate 50 mL of azeite-de-dendê, 50 mL of cooking oil in the pot
3. toss in a full hand of
    - chopped onions
    - chopped peppers
    - chopped tomatoes
4. add a little salt and parsley
5. add the filling when the mixture starts to brown: fish, shrimp, octopus, what have you ...
   if using a frozen fish product, it should have been defrosted by now
6. then 180g de polpa de tomate
7. then 180g de leite de coco

cook for 8 to 10 minutes. when well bubbling, make the pirão (gravy) by taking some of the liquid from the pot and mixing elsewhere with farinha de mandioca and a little leite de coco.

ending note: when i watched his cooks actually making it, they used closer to 100g of polpa de tomate and 300g of leite de coco.

naturally.

www.ingramcontent.com/pod-product-compliance
Lightning Source LLC
Chambersburg PA
CBHW070306120526
44590CB00017B/2580